Clarke Carlisle was born in Preston in 1979, and began his playing career at Blackpool, before moving on to a series of clubs, including Watford and Burnley, both of whom he helped to reach the Premier League, and Queens Park Rangers, where he won three England Under-21 caps. In total, he made more than 500 appearances at senior level.

Carlisle was the chairman of the PFA for three years, and has appeared on both *Countdown* and *Question Time*. He has presented two highly acclaimed documentaries for the BBC: *Is Football Racist?* and *Football's Suicide Secret*. Having retired from the game in 2013, he now works as a pundit for ITV. He lives with his wife and their two young children in Yorkshire, and he has a daughter from a previous relationship.

D0230568

You Don't Know Me, But...
A FOOTBALLER'S LIFE
CLARKE CARLISLE

SIMON &
SCHUSTER

London · New York · Sydney · Toronto · New Delhi

A CBS COMPANY

First published in Great Britain by Simon & Schuster UK Ltd, 2013
This paperback edition published by Simon & Schuster UK Ltd, 2014
A CBS Company

1 3 5 7 9 10 8 6 4 2

Simon & Schuster UK Ltd
1st Floor
222 Gray's Inn Road
London WC1X 8HB

www.simonandschuster.co.uk

Simon & Schuster Australia,
Sydney

Simon & Schuster India,
New Delhi

Every reasonable effort has been made to contact copyright holders of material
reproduced in this book. If any have inadvertently been overlooked, the publishers would
be glad to hear from them and make good in future editions any errors or omissions
brought to their attention.

A CIP catalogue record for this book is available from the British Library

ISBN: 978-1-47112-884-4
Ebook ISBN: 978-1-47112-883-7

Typeset by Hewer Text UK Ltd, Edinburgh
Printed in the UK by CPI (UK) Ltd, Croydon, CR0 4YY

To Gem, Fran, Marley and Honey May,
I love you with all my heart,
Infinity 2012

CONTENTS

— CHAPTER 1 —

GET YOUR TATTS OUT

To tell you the story of a season I should probably start at the beginning, but to give the whole thing some kind of context, I really have to start at the end.

The end of every season is the same, whether it results in glory, failure or mid-table obscurity, there is only one thing on my mind: holidays. We've learnt over the years not to book a holiday in the first two weeks immediately after the season. Why? Because all I do is sleep. I'm sure many people are aware of this phenomenon – where your body seems to shut down when you get a break after a particularly hectic period – and I know it hits most of my team-mates, too. When the season stops, I don't simply have a few lie-ins – I can barely stay awake for most of the day.

Everyone has experienced this feeling in some form or another: mums, dads, businessmen and women the world over. When you have had a really busy time in your life, when you have been working intensely or rushing about all day for a sustained period of time, you don't notice how tired your body is. Somehow you just get through it, because your focus is on the task at hand. It is only when you stop to take a breather, allow your body and mind to switch off, that the fatigue engulfs you. All those ailments that you've batted away for that period just annihilate you and your brain turns to mush, unable to process the simplest of demands. The rigours of a football season aren't just physically demanding; there's an intensity to it all that drains you mentally and emotionally.

Looking back over a team's campaign can paint a picture that in no way reflects the truth. Let's take Northampton Town in the 2011-12 season, for example. From the outside, it looks as though it was a tough start to the year and the club were in a difficult position over Christmas – on New Year's Day the side was at the very bottom of the Football League and were still bumping along at the foot of the table at the start of March – but they achieved safety (if that can be described as an 'achievement') relatively comfortably, thanks to a run of one defeat in nine, which enabled the team to get away with picking up only three points from the last six games.

The reality of being a part of that side was completely different. A team rarely achieves safety when they are bottom of the pile at the turn of the year, and this overriding notion affected everybody's view of what the club could accomplish. Week after week, the press questions were based around this Green Mile that we were walking, and the pressure to produce results was huge. The manager, Aidy Boothroyd, tried to deflect as much of it as he could, fielding responsibility for the situation and results front of house, but in the dressing room it was impossible to avoid the icy tentacles of Conference football that were wrapping around our ankles.

It affected almost everything we did. All week we would

hope that Saturday would be the day that our form changed. In those circumstances, it is so hard to smile and have fun in training, because the air of impending doom is all around. I know this sounds dramatic, but you have to comprehend the number of lives that relegation affects, especially from league football to non-league.

This isn't just a question of player pride and stains on reputations (although they are the primary considerations for a player); there are the jobs of the manager, coaching staff, office staff, groundsmen and cleaners that are under threat. There's the impact on the club's academy, as it would have to reduce the amount of coaches, sessions and therefore opportunity for the local youngsters. There's the impact on secondary and tertiary businesses, such as sponsors, companies that benefit from match-day foot traffic, schools and community projects that have been endorsed by the club and received support through player visits. All of this is at stake, and the responsibility rests on the shoulders of 11 men who take to the pitch on a Saturday afternoon.

When a player is fighting to avoid relegation, a loss can bring such lows that they are inevitably taken home with you, affecting the dynamic in your own house; while wins don't bring the contrasting highs that you would hope because the outcome of the season is far from certain. In the end, it is the final league position that will distinguish between success and failure, not the result of a single game.

So, having been through that experience for the entire time I'd been at Northampton, having joined them on loan at the end of January, it is no exaggeration that I was completely buggered when last season finished and I happily let my body fall into its annual post-traumatic, catatonic state.

When I eventually came round, we headed out in search of some sun and relaxation. Our destination was a family resort in Greece. The children are a little older now, so it's easier to amuse them on aeroplanes and a late night here or there doesn't have disastrous consequences, which meant we could be a little less particular about flights and times. I adore this part of the year for one simple reason: I get to be with my family, uninterrupted, 24/7. Switching off from the rest of the world is bliss at times, especially when you can immerse yourself in your kids and their excitement levels are off the scale. As parents, we always want to find the best resort we can afford, in the nicest part of the world, with the bluest sea, clearest sky and the tastiest food. However, when we get there we soon realise that our kids just want a swimming pool, an inflatable dolphin and ice-cream. They know there is no other time of the year when they can have ice-cream before lunch, and boy do they milk it.

For the most part of my career, my holidays have been along these lines. I was a young father, my eldest daughter Francesca being born back in 1999 when I was 19 years old. This meant that my only taste of a 'lads' holiday' came at the end of my apprenticeship with Blackpool FC. Twelve young men from the seaside embarked on a journey that is imaginatively remembered as 'Tenerife '98'. If I was to go away with any of the boys now, I know that three nights is plenty for a drinking holiday, four gives you a job on your hands, and five means you are coming home in an absolute 'two and eight'.

Our youthful exuberance and utter naivety saw us book a 14-night stay at Columbus Aparthotel on the edge of Veronicas Strip, the party central of Playa de las Americas in

Tenerife. We were earning either £37.50 or £42.50 a week as YTS lads, so we weren't rich, but you didn't need to be when you could buy a one-litre bottle of San Miguel for 190 pesetas and a full English breakfast was 360 pesetas. Just like my kids with their ice-cream, my excitement was off the scale because I knew that this was the only time of the year when I could drink a bottle of San Miguel for breakfast, and boy did *I* milk it.

This was probably one of my first battles with bravado. The night was a success if you got completely banjoed and managed to pull a delectable young lady – even better if she was flying home the next day, because that saved the awkward conversations by the pool the following morning when you both realised just how dark it had been in Soul Train. There were only two of us who managed to go out every night – Steve Longworth (Longy) and myself, and I think Ian Dickinson (Dicko) managed 13 nights. Longy and I are both Leyland lads, and we actually saw it as a badge of honour that we had done the full stint. The fact that we were both skint and ended up mine-sweeping in Bobby's and Busby's on the final two nights only added to the sense of achievement. I vaguely remember playing in a five-a-side tournament put on by Lineker's bar there too. We put two teams in and one of them won, so we ended up parading our prize – a crate of beer – around the pool like it was the Jules Rimet trophy itself.

But as a professional footballer, even when you're on holi-day you can't switch off fully. We're in Greece, it's 36 degrees and there's not a wisp of cloud in the sky. However, I've got my shorts and trainers on, heart-rate monitor with mapping watch (a freebie from Garmin that I managed to scrounge – owt for nowt and I'm there with my wheelbarrow) and off I go running down the dusty roads of Halkidiki. Truth be told, I could quite easily go to the privacy of the air-conditioned gym, but secretly I love it. I could also wear a vest or any kind of top, but I want people to see my tattoos. Narcissistic, I know, but there's no point in lying. Every year, from Tenerife to Dubai, Corfu to Florida, you'll see me running the streets half-naked and making out like it's one of the drawbacks of the job. Thinking about it, it's probably my way of compensating for being a 'non-famous' footballer. Seeing me doing this generally prompts intrigue among fellow holiday makers, who will enquire about what this crazy man is doing running the streets in such heat. I will be forced to tell them that I play football, but obviously as coyly and unassuming as possible.

This is always a moment that can bring conflicting emotions and responses. The majority of people are intrigued and excited: 'Wow, that's amazing!' they will say. But then comes the downside with the question that inevitably follows: 'Are you famous?'

Obviously not . . .

It's a moment that ensures I never get too carried away with myself, but one that I've learnt to brush off after playing outside the Premier League for the majority of my career. I know that my response can be determined by my state of mind at the time. When I'm feeling low or insecure, I'll tell them: 'I've played in the Premier League with . . .' or even just go straight to: 'I was at Leeds United', because everyone's heard of Leeds, even if they did capitulate and tumble down to the third tier, and have taken a while to emerge from the ashes. This time round, I am definitely already starting to question my validity as a pro, because there isn't a mention of Northampton, and I tell people I am a Burnley player. It is strictly true, as I'd been with the Cobblers on loan, while earlier in the season I'd been loaned out to Preston North End.

I am a highly competitive person, and even more so when I'm on my own. Some people need other people to run against, others need a clock; I just need my head. Even when I'm supposed to be going for an easy jog my head will berate me: 'You can run faster than this. Who are you kidding? You're only cheating yourself. I bet you can't beat your record.'

I pile on all this pressure, yet I'm only supposed to be jogging. However, as bad as this may be for structured training, these solo pre-pre-season sessions are hugely beneficial. Invariably I return from holidays in great shape, having annoyed Mrs C with a disciplined diet of salad and fish, run myself into the ground in sweltering temperatures and had a high caffeine intake to increase my metabolism – or that's my theory anyway.

But this time in Halkidiki, not even halfway through my 40-minute run, the voice that usually taunts and cajoles me to the finishing line says something completely different: 'Really?'

'Really what?'

'Are you going to do this again? Really?'

I am shocked. For all the times that I've struggled in football, all the tough seasons, exhausting pre-seasons and holidays that become pre-pre-seasons, I've never questioned whether I *wanted* to do it. My desire was never in doubt, it was just a question of doing what was needed to get me through the current situation. But, for the first time in my career, I am questioning how much I really wanted it. It is the first sign that I might want to retire.

As I try to analyse this thought, I remember the first time I saw a player give up on the game. Squires Gate in Blackpool has never been the most illustrious of training grounds. You're alongside the runway of Blackpool airport, getting deafened at regular intervals by the increasing air traffic (especially since they started running cheap flights to Marbella) and getting whipped by a vicious combination of the Irish Sea breeze and the horizontal rain that it sweeps in off the coast. That being said, it was my first and only professional training ground, so to me it was everything.

Nigel Worthington was the manager and his assistant was the inimitable Mick Hennigan. Mick's desire for football was only surpassed by his disgust at the modern pro's lack of love for the game in comparison. He was so enthusiastic and very old school. He refused to call a loanee or trialist by their name, referring to them only as their club of origin. It seems strange but it actually fitted his style and demeanour. I still don't know whether his calling one player 'Aston Vanilla' was a genuine mistake or a blatant show of dislike for the lad.

It was the beginning of the 1999-00 season and we were tanking around Squires Gate as usual. Suddenly, halfway through a fartlek run, there came a deep groan from somewhere near the back of the group: 'What the fuck am I doing?'

Looking round, I saw David Bardsley stop, walk to his car and drive off. He eventually came back and saw out the rest of that season, but it was to be his last. Apparently, when it's time to retire you just know, and I suddenly fear I may have hit that point.

GET YOUR TATTS OUT

I am 32 years of age, I've been a professional for 15 years now, and, for a guy of moderate ability, I'm delighted with what I've achieved in the game. Exactly three years ago, I was basking in the glory of victory in the Championship play-off final and, not only that, I was Man of the Match at Wembley. I would have run across the Gobi Desert to get fit that summer of 2009 to be ready for the Premier League season that ensued, but that carrot was a distant memory. What am I really running for now?

CHAPTER 2

PARTING IS SUCH SWEET SORROW

What is it with the British weather? No matter what the Met Office predicts, there never seems to be any kind of summer period. Spoilt by the glorious Greek sunshine, we returned to a typical June in Yorkshire: it's raining, windy and barely into double figures at midday. As disappointing as that was for the tan lines, it was fantastic weather to run the streets of West Yorkshire. I don my Ripponden Harriers gear (wearing a vest this time – I'm not mad) and set out on my favourite trails.

There are times on these runs that the scenery just blows you away. Once you get away from the beaten track, away from the buzz of the M62 and all the 4x4s belonging to the countryside commuters, there are moments when I look around in awe. The rolling hills and expansive moors are a genuine sight to behold. The moment soon passes, though. As I pump my veteran legs one in front of the other up some disgusting inclines, my heartbeat starts to thunder in my ears. A metallic taste from my overworked lungs starts to rise in my throat, as the lactate begins to course through my veins.

I'm desperately seeking the crest of the hill, knowing that once I get there it is downhill all the way, still three miles to home, but downhill nevertheless. Why on earth am I running up these ridiculous hills? My stride has become a step and anyone watching me would be forgiven for thinking I was taking a leisurely stroll, if it wasn't for the award-winning gurn on my face and the sudden attack of the Radcliffes on my head. Finally, I reach the top and my stride starts to lengthen. It's only the natural effect of gravity when running on a decline, but it still manipulates the mind into thinking that the body is strong. My heart rate settles to a manageable 168 and my mind can return to normal thought.

I am currently facing a choice between playing for Northampton Town, the team I had helped to narrowly avoid relegation from the Football League, or Burton Albion. The club where Nigel Clough began his managerial career had barely escaped from the same precarious position as Northampton, finishing three places above us in 17th position. Not only that, the remuneration that was on offer from both clubs meant we would be falling off a financial cliff.

Now don't get me wrong; Northampton's offer of £1500 per week is an excellent income in general terms, and it dwarfed Burton's £800 per week, but when you've been on £8000 per week the season before, it was going to be a hit. I knew that this day would come, when the natural curve of a player's income would take a downward turn, but I had always expected it to be a curve, not a vertical line. My wife and I had set our target for this contract to be £2500 a week. It was a figure that would ensure we could pay all the bills

11

that were coming in, and still be eligible for the mortgage on a property we were looking to buy. I thought it was a realistic figure, especially when I considered what I should already have had in place for this season. However, the last campaign hadn't gone to plan.

Leaving Preston North End early hurt me in two ways: it hurt my pride and it hurt my employment security. I had signed a season-long loan with Preston at the beginning of the 2011-12 season. Eddie Howe was my manager at Burnley and he told me that I would not be playing for them that campaign. He said that he was looking to build a squad of players who were mostly in their mid-twenties, and he also explained that he would not be renewing my contract at the end of the year, either.

I was almost in tears on the other side of the desk. A couple of months earlier, after Burnley had just missed out on a play-off place the season after being relegated from the Premier League, we had discussed the possibility of a new contract and I had been under the impression that I was definitely a part of Eddie's plans. This apparent U-turn was so painful that I didn't have the wherewithal to react. I calmly wished Eddie the best of luck for the new season, jumped in my car and drifted home in a haze of uncertainty.

Burnley was, without doubt, the best, most successful, most enjoyable and closest-knit club that I have ever been at. As players we had risen from Championship relegation favourites to the heights of the Premier League, all via a League Cup semi-final against Tottenham Hotspur and the most monumental day at Wembley. Our wives had formed a friendship that I haven't seen at any other club before or since, and we all felt comfortable in each other's company. I didn't want to hear this news.

What made it even worse was that Eddie didn't even want me to come back for pre-season. He said that I could if I wanted, and I could do what I wanted, but I would no longer be required to attend. What had I done that meant I wasn't even wanted around the place? I don't think I'm a bad egg. I am not unprofessional around the club, and I don't bad-mouth people or sit on the bitter bus, so I didn't understand why I was being kept at arm's length. I tried to be a good example to the younger pros at the club and, if anything I did wasn't becoming of a professional, I made sure to let them know. I spent so much time with lads such as Adam Kay, Alex MacDonald and Jay Rodriguez, all of whom I have a great fondness for and huge admiration of their ability. The club knew that they could trust me, and that I would bring anything to the table and do all I could to help and guide the younger ones. I felt that surely my input in that regard was worth keeping around a football club. It really was the worst way to have to leave a club: unwanted.

It's in the nature of a football career that players leave clubs for many different reasons, and it's actually very rare that it is down to personal choice. When I left Blackpool back in May 2000, I was being sold from a Division 3 club (we had just been relegated from Division 2) to a Division 1 side. Not only that, but I was going to Queens Park Rangers, a team that had relatively recently been relegated from the Premier League and were tipped for a swift return. This type of move fills you with joy, excitement, anticipation and a great deal of anxiety. How will I settle? Will I be good enough? Will the players rate and accept me? Ultimately, though, the overriding feeling is one of achievement and hope. To know that your qualities have been watched, assessed and deemed sufficient enough for a club to spend a quarter of a million pounds on you is immensely satisfying, as is the increase in salary. I went from earning £26,000 a year to £125,000 a year, and boy did I enjoy it!

That move happened after the end of the season, so I never went back in to Blackpool. I didn't call my team-mates to say goodbye, go for one last night out or have any kind of leaving party, I just upped and left. Knowing what I do now, I would have done things slightly differently, but there is a distinct lack of appreciation of what a club and its staff have done for you when you're that age. At 20 years old, I was drawn to the lights of London and the allure of potential success like a moth to a lamp, and I dizzied myself around that town's perpetual glow for four years, but more of that later.

A footballer can leave a club for a number of personal reasons, too. You often see this when an overseas player fails to settle in this country and he gets homesick, missing the safety net of family, friends and familiar surroundings. This very same notion can happen with British-born players moving to a different region. Oftentimes London lads can't cope with the slower-paced life out in the sticks, and even more common is the situation where it is the other way round. It was the fast-paced 24/7 lifestyle of London that I couldn't cope with, generally due to my inability to say no to a pint or a party. I found the constant temptation of London's West End a little overwhelming. I felt that I needed to move back up north, closer to my family network, in order to fully implement a recovery programme from the difficulties I got myself into.

CHAPTER 3

MEET MR MEDAL WINNER

nother reason people end up moving is when they just don't see eye to eye with the manager. A football club is like any other workplace; the likelihood of you and your boss getting on is a veritable lottery. Even when a manager buys a player, and so he is 'his' purchase, unless they've worked together before it's impossible to know whether their personalities, egos or opinions will clash.

I have worked under 13 different managers in my time in football, and that sort of clash happened only once. The man in question was Kevin Blackwell at Leeds United. On leaving Queens Park Rangers in 2004, I couldn't have wished for a better opportunity than to join Leeds. What a huge club! I was gobsmacked by the ground, the training facilities and the ardent support of their fans. I hadn't seen the likes of any of these before in my career.

I flew back from Tenerife halfway through a family holiday as soon as I received the phone call. I had made my decision to leave QPR, even though they had offered me a fantastic contract to stay. A four-year deal on over £4000 per week would have been utterly amazing at the time, but my decision was based on personal welfare, not financial gain. Just how much that was the case can be shown by the fact that Kevin Blackwell offered me £2500 per week and sternly told me that there was no room for manoeuvre. He also gave me a dressing-down about my drinking and told me that no one else would touch me with a barge pole; he made out as though he was doing me a favour.

As it happened, I had the offer from QPR and I had also spoken to Neil Warnock at Sheffield United. They had offered an identical figure to Leeds, and I must admit that I found Warnock an altogether more personable guy. However, having set my stall out to move up north and been given two phenomenal options, there was only ever one winner. Leeds had been relegated from the Premier League that season, and had been in the Champions League semi-final as recently as 2001 – this was a huge club and I was desperate to be a part of that.

The year that I spent at Leeds was a taste of big-club football, but also a taste of big-club egos. There were some attitudes at the club that stank to high heaven. Given the financial troubles that the club faced at that time, perhaps Blackwell wanted to give the fans and everyone associated with Leeds some hope when he declared himself in the press as 'the saviour'. But really that was the moment when alarm bells should have started ringing. We had a laugh about it in the dressing room, because we thought he was way out of his depth in the situation he found himself in.

Blackwell was certainly an immensely qualified coach, having worked under the likes of Warnock and Peter Reid. However, this was his first managerial role, having been the assistant manager the previous season, and it would have been a huge challenge even for a much more experienced man. Unfortunately, he did not have the wherewithal to deal with such strong characters as Paul Butler, Sean Gregan, Gary Kelly, Michael Duberry and Seth Johnson among others. Even the young pros such as Matthew Kilgallon seemingly had him 'on toast'.

It wasn't the fact that he didn't have the full respect of the changing room that riled me, though, as that can take time – especially for someone who has been promoted from within, as both sides get used to the new roles. What annoyed me more was that as far as I was concerned he came across as discourteous, arrogant and over-confident. There's no doubt that you need a certain level of grandiosity and presence to manage a club like Leeds, but that doesn't mean you should be tactless to others – especially some of the support staff. The kitman, Sean Hardy, was one of the best and hardest working kitmen I have had the pleasure of working with, but he often appeared to get the treatment for little obvious reason. Physio Alan Sutton is possibly the nicest man you could meet, and had been at the club for aeons, but he was regularly hauled over by the boss. Sometimes we would be in the middle of an excellent training session and he would interrupt things by saying to his coach: 'No, no, no. This isn't what I want. Go over and take the kids.'

If it was meant to impress the players that Blackwell was now in charge, it often had the opposite effect. Despite all this, and the problems the club faced, he was initially quite popular with the fans and we ended up in mid-table in the Championship after his first campaign. But the final straw for me came in the 2005-06 pre-season. After being told by the lads that Blackwell had held a meeting in which he had stated that I would never play for Leeds again, I started to look for a new club. When the first day of training came around, he told me that he had said no such thing and all 36 lads were mistaken. So back to training I went and was feeling very good. We were doing a skills session one hot July day when Sean Gregan volleyed the ball away on the whistle.

'Go and get it, Clarke,' said Blackwell, so I started to walk over.

'Fucking quicker,' he added, so I broke into a boxer's jog or 'bobble' as it's known.

'When I say run, you fucking *run*,' he bellowed.

'I am running,' I replied.

'You need to do as I say. You fucking owe me. I saved your career!'

'You what? You didn't save anything.'

'I saved you bringing you here, if you don't like it then fuck off.'

So I did. I walked straight back to the dressing rooms. He shouted something to me from across the pitch but I didn't turn around, I just threw him the bird, high over my head, and carried on walking. Anyone who knows me will tell you that I am not a man for confrontation, and do anything to avoid it, but I had had enough and knew it was time to move on.

As luck would have it, only two years later I came across Blackwell again, when I was on loan at Luton Town while recovering from a long-term injury. He came in to replace the sacked Mike Newell and there weren't two unhappier people in the whole of Luton than myself and Matthew Spring, who had also been privy to his antics at Leeds. I must say that he was a completely different animal for the remaining three weeks that I was there. He greeted me like we were long-lost friends and seemed to listen and value my opinion. I was astonished, but I know that people can change – after all, I have changed a lot myself over the years. Too much too soon is a phrase often applied to players who move to big clubs, but I think it can also apply to managers. Maybe the Leeds job was too large a mantle for him as his first full-time appointment and he learnt much from it. I hope so, and certainly the signs were that he had.

The greatest outcome of my time at Leeds was that I met my next manager, Aidy Boothroyd, the coach who the players felt was being undermined by Blackwell. Before that season was out, he was given a fantastic chance as manager at Watford, taking up the reins in March 2005. A few months later, with my career at Leeds clearly over, the club had given me permission to talk to Stoke City. While I was on my way down to speak to them, Aidy called: 'Don't sign anything, just come and talk to us first.'

If it hadn't been him, and if we hadn't spent the last year cursing together, I wouldn't have even made the trip, but it was, and I am glad that I did. We went on to win promotion to the Premier League that season and, by some beautiful twist of fate, we beat Kevin Blackwell and Leeds United in the play-off final at the Millennium Stadium. I wish I could say that I was gracious in victory, but I can't. I sprinted over to Blackwell at the final whistle, shook his hand and whispered 'fuck you' in his ear. It really shouldn't have been as enjoyable as it was.

Another reason a player leaves a club – and it is probably the hardest to deal with – is because the manager simply doesn't appear to rate you. This was the case I faced with Eddie Howe at Burnley, and it was something that had happened to me only once before. It happened, oddly enough, when Aidy let me go from Watford because he said I was too slow. He told me that while my colleagues in the centre of defence may have made more mistakes than I did, they at least had the pace to rectify them. At 28 years of age, this was the first time I'd been told that I wasn't good enough.

I was supposedly in the prime of my life, at the peak of my career, but apparently not. It really hurt me. I even started to think about retirement, about re-education and new opportunities. Most of all, I started to judge myself. I let Aidy's opinion about my footballing ability define me as a person. I was quiet, morose and moody around the house. I dwelled on what I'd achieved in the game, on what might have been and what the hell the future had in store. I was low, especially because this was a judgement that came from someone I liked and respected; had it come from someone else where the relationship was less warm, it would have been easier to dismiss.

But my despair changed one August night when I reported to Vicarage Road for a League Cup first round tie. The gaffer pulled me aside and told me he'd accepted an offer from Burnley. He didn't want me to play in the game just in case I got injured and I was free to go. I turned around, got in the car and drove up to East Lancashire the next morning. When I got there, manager Steve Cotterill didn't mess about.

'Clarkey, this is all I'm offering. I can't do any more, we're not a rich club but we're a good club.'

Little did he know that the offer of three years on £5000, £5500 then £6000 per week was far and away the best contract of my career to that point. I would happily have signed for much less. Lancashire is my home county, we could split the difference between there and Leeds (where

Mrs C hails from) and buy a property nearby. What was more, I had the offer of regular football and I was coming home to roost. In fact, I was about to embark on the most fruitful period of my career, and the best was yet to come.

The difference between then and now, as I consider my options between Northampton and Burton, is that I no longer have time on my side. I know that I am on the wrong side of 30 and that my ability is deteriorating with age. The industry is beginning to tighten its purse strings and squad sizes are smaller, contracts are shorter and salaries are lower. Even my own faith in my ability to prove yet another manager wrong is dwindling, so why would anyone else believe in me? I could hang around for the last year of my contract and see if Eddie Howe gets binned, but it's highly unlikely. Burnley is a very stable club. Managers aren't removed on a whim like at so many other places. Plus, my stock would be even lower if I spent a year in the wilderness doing nothing. I am not the type of guy who can just sit around and pick up a wage. I need to be wanted, I need to be appreciated and I need to play.

Once the decision was made to leave Burnley in the summer of 2011, there was no leaving do or farewell send-off. The nature of the industry is that players come and go on a regular basis. There is very little sentiment involved when a team-mate moves on. If the change occurs during the course of the season, then a player might come in and say his good-byes with hugs and handshakes all round. Generally, however, when you go to speak to another club, you sign for them that day, which means that you have to report to training with your new team-mates the next day. There's no time to be sentimental, it's straight down to work. The majority of the guys you were playing with the day before will never be spoken to again, and that's just how it is.

When Phil Brown called me and asked to meet for a chat, I jumped at the chance. The last time I had met him face to face was as a 16-year-old kid. I was playing for Blackpool 'A' team at the weekend and Phil was Sam Allardyce's assistant with the first team. Ever since then, he has emerged from Sam's shadow and was front and centre of Hull's promotion to the Premier League. I'd had no direct contact with him, so, like many others, my main points of reference were his on-pitch dressing-down of Hull at half time and his sere-nade of the Hull fans the season they stayed up in the Premier League. Furthermore, he has that all-year tan that smacks of the electric beach and has a level of confidence that a lot of people cannot handle.

With all this in mind, I was expecting to have a meeting with a bar of Dairy Milk. (When someone loves themselves so much that they would eat themselves, we refer to them as chocolate, and that is what I was expecting to sit across from me at the Turnpike in Ripponden.) What I actually met was so impressive that I felt a tad guilty about my pre-concep-tion. Phil Brown is a confident man. He is confident in his ability, he is assured about his destination and he is deter-mined in his approach. He talked to me incisively about the state of me, my career, Preston North End and their predica-ment. He spoke with conviction about how he would change that and, crucially, he listened to my opinions on all of the above. I drove home flabbergasted that I could be so wrong about someone, so much so that Gem wouldn't even believe me when I told her. That said, I had sufficient experience of football to know that a man is defined by his actions, so I would have to see if he could fulfil his words, but whatever the case he is an outstanding orator.

I was so convinced by his pitch that not only did I sign a season-long loan, I also signed a pre-contract agreement that would see me stay at Preston for a year after the loan, on a wage of £4000 per week. I didn't actually need 'convincing' per se, to sign for Preston. It was my hometown club and many of my schoolmates had been going to Deepdale for years. It had been a source of constant ridicule that I had played for Blackpool. Perhaps because of that, the M55 derby was invariably when I played my best games for Blackpool. Not only did I want to silence my mates in the Town End, but I also wanted to punish my local club for never seemingly showing an interest in me. The moment they did, however, I jumped at the chance and left all chants of 'Sea-Sea-Sea-siders' way behind.

The 2011-12 campaign at Preston started extremely well. Phil Brown had really bought into the military mentality, after a pre-season jaunt with the Commandos. Each month was given a mission title like 'Operation Sandbag', and he made a 10ft banner with images of the guys toiling up dunes with 20kg bags on their backs, hoping to garner the spirit and determination that was required to complete that task and apply it to the forthcoming fixtures. While we were winning it was great: morale was high and Phil and his assistant, Brian Horton (affectionately known as Nobby), were all smiles.

It all started to unravel one Saturday down at Leyton Orient. We were on an unbelievable run – we'd recorded seven wins in a row to push ourselves up towards the top of the League 1 table. Iain Hume and Neil Mellor were flying up top, being pushed all the way by Jamie Proctor. Paul Coutts and Danny Mayor were supplying the ammo, while Graham 'Grezza' Alexander, Craig Morgan and I were the defensive steel. Then we were beaten 2-1 at Brisbane Road, deservedly so, but after our recent form I didn't feel there was any need to panic. Nobby, on the other hand, thought otherwise.

He lost it in the dressing room, effing and blinding and waving his notes around like a composer's baton. I don't mind a bit of fire every now and again, but I think it has to be constructive. This is something that was very much missing from Nobby's dressing-down. This was shit, that was shit and it seemed that the fault lay entirely with anyone under 20 years of age. I hate it when managers and coaches do this. Sometimes they justifiably feel the need to shout at people, but perhaps they don't have the balls to nail the senior players. Instead, they'll go overboard on a seemingly trivial mistake by a younger player and skim over the senior player's contribution.

It has to be the other way around in my opinion. I was 32 years old at the time and had played nearly 500 games, while Grezza had played over 1000 games, so if you are going to scream and shout, do it at us! We can take it, we can extrapolate the information from the tirade instead of just feeling the emotional barrage like a lot of younger players do. The ironic thing is that the manager/coach would actually gain more respect if they did nail a senior pro and call them to task. All players want is honesty. We know when we've been good, we know when we've been crap, just be honest and fair and we'll be the same back.

Whatever the intention, it didn't work: we picked up just one point from our next nine games. For some reason, our whole training regime descended into some kind of lucky dip.

We embarked on three of the worst sessions of my career. The first was when we had to run the steps of the stadium.

Phil brought us in on a Sunday morning after a defeat and decided to punish us for it. Under the guise of 'mental strength', he sent us up and down every step in Deepdale. I hadn't done a session like it since 1997, and that's because it's ridiculous. We had another game in two days, but that was immaterial. 'Tiredness is a state of mind,' he told us, which it can be, but muscle fatigue is a scientific fact, which is what my calves and hamstrings told me in a far louder and more convincing voice. We completed the task like we always did, but the morale of the squad took a severe hit.

If that wasn't bad enough, a week later we found ourselves Greco-Roman wrestling on mats at our Springfields training ground. Led by our psychological guru Mike Farrell, a guy who had been working with Wigan Warriors and someone I really liked as a person, we started throwing each other around the gym. Footballers really are like lemmings. For all of the murmurs and grumblings of discontent, we just do as we're told and, due to the basic competitive nature that is ubiquitous among footballers, we do it to win. No surprise then when our goalkeeper, Ian Turner, broke his toes. I wondered how the club would reveal the circumstances under which such a huge blow was dealt to the squad. A 'training injury' just didn't cut it for us, but apparently was sufficient for prying ears.

With combat sports taken out of the equation, but with plenty of aggression seemingly needing to be vented, we went where no other session had taken me before: punching inanimate objects. In pairs and standing either side of a ruddy great big tractor tyre, we had to punch it one-handed and knock the thing over. Ludicrous! Having said that, I took great delight in being undefeated at the task, but that doesn't take away from how terrible the session was. In between these sessions, Phil and Nobby's moods seemed to veer wildly: one day there would be smiles, the next day frowns, the next would be silent treatment and after that, well, who knew.

They left the club shortly after, which I was unhappy about. Even if the reality of working under Phil Brown didn't completely match the sales pitch, there were signs that it was possible to get there. We had enough good players in the squad to be successful, but injuries to Iain Hume and Neil Mellor had been a major contributory factor to the downturn in our form, and their imminent return would have been a huge shot in the arm. On top of that, I always believe a manager should be given at least one full season. Unless the club is rooted to the foot of the table and well adrift, there is always time and opportunity for things to turn around, especially if you've seen it work already.

With the rumour mill going crazy about the vacancy, the players' choice (or at least this player's choice) was Graham Alexander. He took temporary charge with David Unsworth and there was a palpable shift in atmosphere around the place. Both guys were respected by the squad for their playing prowess, and both seemed to have a philosophy about the managerial side of the game that we could buy into.

Instead, the job went to a man who I knew little about: Graham Westley. He had a good record with his previous club, Stevenage Borough, taking them from non-league to League 1 in four years, which was an outstanding achievement. The stories we'd heard about his methods were a little disconcerting, however. One or two of those who had played for him described him as a dictatorial leader who trains his players from nine to five. They believed he was more concerned about how much you can bench-press rather than your passing stats. Despite the stories, I decided to go into this new regime with an open mind to see what lay in store.

When a new manager enters a club, the first impression he creates is of great importance, especially if he doesn't have a big profile that precedes him. The players want to feel that he is the right man to lead them to victory, someone who knows what he is talking about and who will inspire the team to move forward together, conquering all in our way. It may sound a little idealistic, and perhaps it conjures images of some great war-cry or Al Pacino's speech in *Any Given Sunday*, but it's true: the squad needs to be convinced and the first meeting goes a long way to determining how quickly that will happen.

GW (as he referred to himself in his text messages) was due to take control on the Monday, but introduced himself to the squad on the Saturday before the game. We were all called into the Invincibles Players' Lounge at 12.30 and told to await the new manager's arrival. The rumour was that Westley had been appointed, but a lot of us refused to believe it, mainly because we'd heard about his working week and hoped to avoid that. Then GW strode into the room along with his assistant, Dino Maamria, and addressed the lads. I really liked what he had to say. His ethos sounded good, his reasoning was logical and his record was successful. Then, in one statement, it all came crumbling down.

'My kids don't call me "Dad", they call me "Medal Winner".'

I was sick in my mouth. I heard a few giggles and chuckles from behind me and a look of pure disbelief on the face of one of my team-mates. I waited to see if there was an element of humour in the statement, but sadly there didn't appear to be any. At that moment, the chance of a good first impression was gone. He opened the floor to any questions and I put up my hand: 'Can we go and get ready? We've got a game in an hour.'

It wasn't meant to be facetious, but it was greeted with laughter by the guys behind me.

We went into the working week having been told that we would be working until 4.30pm every day apart from Friday, when it would be until around 2pm. We were given a questionnaire all about us to fill in. We were asked to list our strengths, weaknesses, hopes and aspirations, vital stats and then to add anything else we thought might be relevant. After being told by GW that he worked on 'brutal honesty', my AOB probably gave him more to think about than he'd bargained for. It read:

'I am a recovering alcoholic, gambling addict and depression-suffering smoker. I am apprehensive about your new regime but will give it everything I've got.'

Well, he might as well know the truth up front.

I have experienced many different styles of management in my career, and the successful ones have varied dramatically. With that in mind, I will always give a new regime the chance to show its merits. Mr Westley's methods were of a type that I had never witnessed before, and doubt I will again. The working week was long and hard. It seemed to me as though the plan was to make Saturday the easiest session of the week, which has a warped sense of logic to it. If training was so hard that Saturday was a respite, then you should easily be able to deal with the physical requirements of a season of football.

Where I felt this plan had a huge stumbling block was that he expected us to adapt to his regime immediately. It doesn't happen; most footballers are used to training sessions that run from about 10am to 1pm, and sometimes not even that long. If you are going to double the workload, there needs to be a transition period where players can become acclimatised to the new levels of exertion. I don't believe he allowed for that, and I told him so. Brutal honesty.

We also had to put up with regular comparisons with 'my boys', by which he meant his former team at Stevenage. Using their levels as a stick to beat us with was a bad tactic; they had been working like this for three or four years. I have no doubts that the squad at Preston would have reached those fitness levels after a good few months of training, and as we were better players technically, we would have become a better team.

GW didn't agree, though; he appeared to believe that compromise was weakness and transitions should be immediate, which was very short-sighted in my opinion. After he had been at the club for a little over a fortnight, he called me in for a meeting after an away trip to Yeovil, a game we lost 2-1 in which I scored our consolation goal. He didn't believe that I could commit 100 per cent to what he was asking of his squad at Deepdale, due to my extra-curricular commitments. I told him I didn't agree, that I had tapered my work accordingly and would continue to give all that I have.

Not seeing me as part of his plans past that season, Westley asked if we could terminate my loan agreement. I agreed for two reasons. Firstly, I hate being somewhere where I'm not wanted. It takes all of the enjoyment away from what is a fantastic environment. Secondly, I found it the worst regime I had ever worked under. I was being coached to move outside of my full-back when he's defending one v one, which was the complete opposite of everything I'd been taught for 30 years.

Westley's assistant, Dino, seemed to prefer a confrontational style of motivation on and off the pitch; he saw the number of crunching tackles we made in a game as a key way of judging how well it had gone. What's more, the training sessions were dragged out to fill the time, instead of focusing on the session's needs. For example, one afternoon we had finished our shape and pattern-of-play work, but it was still only 4.05. So GW sent us on a couple of laps around the pitch and then made us do sit-ups and press-ups in a big puddle. When the lads tried to move to a drier part of the ground, he squashed us all in together and barked out for more reps.

There was no opportunity to switch off either. Once we got home at around 6.30, he would send us random texts; the latest I received was at just before 2am! I am not sure I could have coped with that intensity for too long, so I agreed to the termination, and with it went my contract for the 2012-13 season, too. It was never officially revoked in writing by Preston, so I could have dragged them through the courts for my money if I'd wanted to be an arse, but I'm not. Despite all this, we still got into a row after I'd left, but it was time to move on. And, indeed, it would be for GW as well, as he lost his job at the club midway through the following season when performances didn't improve.

— CHAPTER 4 —

THE BEST DAY IN THE CALENDAR

The season is less than a month away and I haven't signed for anyone. It has been such a relief to be able to relax and enjoy my summer. I haven't done much running or gym work, I've been eating like a normal person and it feels great. With my old contract now at an end, this is my first week as an officially unemployed man, which feels quite surreal. I've always had a very structured life: football dictates where you should be and when, what you should eat, how you should cook it and even what you should wear most of the time, so to be outside of this framework is really bizarre.

I was hoping to have had some media work sewn up by now. After presenting a documentary on racism in football for BBC3 last year, I received a lot of positive feedback and several enquiries about the possibility of doing future work in this area. Now I need some of those to come through. It's great being able to get up at midday and pick up the kids from school, but without a focus for my daily attentions I feel very lost. Not only that, I have been so thriftless throughout my life that we don't have a 'rainy day' pot to fall back on. We need a regular income if we're going to continue to

31

live where we are. There's only so much *Loose Women* that a man can take before he starts to lose his mind. I need to get to work for more reasons than just money.

This is the first pre-season that I've missed since 1996. I genuinely believed that I would be able to make the transition this summer from football to the media, but I am sadly mistaken. I'm discovering just how hard it is to get work in the real world. This is a very harsh lesson to learn. I've found out that compliments and statements of intent don't necessarily translate into guaranteed work.

It's 12 August 2012, the season starts this coming weekend and I have lost the two opportunities that I had with Northampton and Burton because I wanted them to pay me more than they were able to offer. I wanted to be able to sign for a club on my terms, and still believed that I had the wherewithal to achieve that. I was wrong. I was confident I could push them hard because I believed all the hype that was coming from people about my opportunity in the media, too. I thought that I would have a plethora of options to go with if I ended up without a club and so retired from the game. I was wrong. Not only is the media industry saturated in the 'ex-pro' department, the remuneration is vastly different to what can be earned on the pitch. No work in the pipeline, no doors open in the game and a set of bills to be paid in a couple of weeks – bills that were built on a handsome salary that has quickly become a distant memory. I need to pull a rabbit out here, or at the very least my finger.

Talk about landing on your feet! I just pimped myself out via the medium of *Soccer AM*. Thank you, Hels Bells and Max. After watching the opening round of fixtures last week,

I realised what a monumental error I had made. There are few better days in the football calendar for all footballers than the first match of the season. You have worked your nuts off for six to eight weeks, running around tracks, up and down dale, playing friendlies in Asia, America and Altrincham, all preparing yourself for this day. It doesn't matter what happened the season before, it doesn't matter what the press think, what the supporters say or what any other team does. Today is the moment of opportunity for every team in the land. You walk out in front of a packed ground, no matter what the league. The roar goes up and sends a shiver down your spine. This is it. What are we going to do this season? What can we achieve? It all starts here: hopes and dreams are brought to the altar and offered up to the footballing gods for them to cast their die.

There are two opening days that really stick out in my mind. The first one was for Blackpool in the 1998-99 season. I didn't even play, but the memory of walking out at Maine Road in front of over 32,000 is indelibly imprinted on my memory. I was an 18-year-old boy and this was mind-blowing. The roar of the crowd that day is something I'll never forget. The second one was when we took the field for Burnley against Stoke at the Britannia Stadium in 2009. We walked out on to that pitch as Premier League players and that felt so very good. After having thought I was going home to roost when I moved to Burnley, this surpassed all my hopes and dreams.

For the first time I can remember, it was actually raining on opening day. It is usually baking hot; no matter what the weather has been like for the entirety of pre-season, you can usually guarantee that the first game of the season will take your dehydration levels to a new high, but not this year. I wondered if it was some sort of pathetic fallacy, a reflection of the plot to my life story: the one time it might have been easy to play, I didn't even have a team to play for.

Mrs C and I take the kids to Birstall to look around Toys R Us as it is Marley's birthday in a couple of months. It takes every ounce of self-control I can muster to stay away from the vidiprinter on my phone. I have no allegiance to any club now, or indeed to football, but the temptation is all-consuming. As soon as we set foot back in the house, I have *Soccer Saturday* on the box. How are Northampton doing? Burnley? QPR? Leeds? Watford? Blackpool? Burton? Bloody Burton! I haven't even played for them, but I already have a dose of the 'What ifs?' I am a footballer who can still play: what am I doing trawling around shopping centres and watching the results come in? I need to play. I need to get a club.

I called Aidy; it's too late. I called Gary Rowett; too late. I called every manager or assistant whose number I had in my phone book: Micky Mellon at Fleetwood, Barry Fry at Posh, Leon Hunter at Stevenage, John Ward at Colchester, Graham Turner at Shrewsbury, Alan Knill at Scunthorpe, Brian Carey at Doncaster; I was too late for them all. What the hell do I do now? As luck would have it, I got a call from Chris Nutbeam of the *Soccer AM* team to see if I would come on the show the next weekend.

This was a perfect opportunity for me to put out one final plea for employment. *Soccer AM* and *Soccer Saturday* are the two bastions of modern-day football TV. Everyone watches them – so much so that even Mrs C watches them when I'm not there. They are part of the Saturday routine. All players want to see themselves on Showboat on a Saturday morning, or practise hitting the crossbar from the halfway line for when the cameras are in town, and no one wants to have a taxi called for them! I knew I wouldn't have a better opportunity to tell the football community that I still wanted to play, so I took it.

A couple of days later, I received a call from Gary Mills, the manager at York City, asking if I'd be interested in having a chat. I was over there like a shot. We were both very honest with each other. He had two centre-halves injured and needed someone in quick. He offered me £1000 per week plus £100 per appearance and a £100 clean-sheet bonus. I told him I just wanted to get back in the door, playing football, and that we could go from there. We agreed that I would sign until the end of December so that we would both have the opportunity to see if it worked and we could then make a longer-term decision at a later date. I have never been so happy to accept a drop in wages amounting to 87.5 per cent – after all, it is far better than a 100 per cent reduction.

After a brief interlude, my career is once again active. It is 29 August 2012 and I'm a Minsterman. I do hope I've made the right decision. Let's see what tomorrow brings.

CHAPTER 5

HOW TO CREATE A GOOD FIRST IMPRESSION

My first day at York should be a breeze. It's my eighth or ninth club and I'm 32 years of age, so why do I feel so nervous? To be honest, nervous doesn't even cut it; it's far deeper than that.

My alarm went off at 6am and the excitement of what was before me should have meant that I jumped out of bed like it was Christmas morning. Negative. Four snooze-button hits later and I've got about three minutes to get ready and arrive at the train station. It could be construed as a warning sign by some, but it just reflects the place that I'm currently in. If you've suffered from depression before, you will be familiar with the feeling that no amount of sleep is ever enough. Even after a full ten hours and an afternoon nap, the evening can't come quickly enough. When it does you have an excuse to go to bed again so that you can escape the realities of the world and the hideously illogical way that your mind processes them, which makes things even worse.

Hauled out of bed by Mrs C, I get to the station and board the train just in time, bound for pastures new. I double-checked that York was the end of the line, which it was, and promptly fell asleep. I reach my destination with a good 45 minutes to spare before I have to be at the ground for my medical, so I buy a coffee and sit down at the station entrance, staring up at the big clock above the doorway. My mind is full of questions and doubts.

'Should I be doing this?'

'Will I be fit enough?'

'Should I just go home?'

'Should I just disappear?'

I sit there contemplating what the hell has happened over two and a half years that have seen me dropping from the Premier League to League 2 newcomers, and on a short-term contract. I wasn't even worth a full year. The worst bit about it is that I know I am soon going to have to stand in front of the press and lie through my teeth with the usual new-signing bullshit. But in truth, what hurts me the most is that this is my only option. There's no hiding it in this situation. However I word it, the footballing world is going to see that I am on my arse and I am grateful for this olive branch being offered by Gary Mills.

Not all first days are like this. I remember walking down the long, dark corridor at Turf Moor stadium. I was delighted to get away from Watford because Aidy Boothroyd had told me I was too slow for his team and that I wouldn't play that year. Steve Cotterill made it clear that he rated me and so I waltzed down the corridor to meet my new compatriots. I had my bag of boots, trainers, shin pads and all the other gear a footballer needs and I thought I'd drop them in the boot room as I went past.

The boot room at Turf Moor is basically a dingy, smelly closet under the stand. It has a sloping roof so you can stand fully upright only in the first few feet of the room, then you have to limbo to get your boots if they're on the far wall. Because I haven't got a squad number yet, I just place my boots on the floor. I don't want to upset anyone by taking their space, not on my first day.

Suddenly the room went black and, not being fond of dark, confined spaces, I turned to see if the guys had locked the new boy in, or played some original prank like that. Well, to say I got a fright is an understatement. I turned around to see 14 stones of unadulterated muscle mass filling the doorway. Just to make it worse, they belonged to a guy who I had previous with, one Ade Akinbiyi.

Ade is renowned for his aggressive style on the pitch, and his volcanic temper. I had used this against him in games by trying to wind him up and affect his concentration. The logic is that if he's thinking about me and where I am, he's not thinking about the ball. Therefore, nipping, shirt-pulling, body checks and blatant trips were the order of the day. On a football pitch, with the protection of the referee, linesmen and ten team-mates, I felt fine. Cornered in unfamiliar territory with this beast blocking my only exit, I didn't. To add to my fear and anxiety, the last time we'd faced each other the entire Burnley squad had had to hold Ade back while he threatened to shoot me, and Gifton Noel-Williams (another man mountain) was trying to climb over the mêlée screaming that he'd get me! It was all part of the usual 'handbags' that can occasionally flare up in the tunnel.

Of all the situations where I have been beaten up, this looked like being the smelliest location and definitely the most severe kicking I would get. While I debated whether to kick him in the 'town halls' or just get on my knees and pray, the biggest smile I have ever seen flashed across Ade's face. He must have sensed my apprehension because he burst out laughing and threw his arms out, saying: 'Bring it in big man, welcome to Burnley.' The sense of relief was matched only by the weight of my drawers.

It's now 8.45 at York station, so I'd better get a shift-on. No matter what my reservations are, the truth is that this is my only offer of guaranteed income, so I need to get on with it and stop worrying.

The day went as comfortably as I could expect. York enjoyed great success last season, winning the FA Trophy and the Conference play-offs to get back into league football. With it being a former league club, last having played at this level in 2004, Bootham Crescent ground was tidy enough, but the training facilities were extremely basic. A couple of big metal Portakabins in a field made it a real throwback to my beginnings at Blackpool. I wasn't in any position to complain, and nor would I, but the fact that the heaters weren't working and the showers were broken and mouldy showed just how far away from the dizzy heights I had come.

My only other concern was that the manager had seemingly elected to throw me straight into the team. Oh my fooking life! I haven't done a jot of proper training for over two months and the 45 minutes that we did today had my chest heaving. I genuinely don't know how I'm going to cope with an actual match. Luckily, I am one of those fortunate players whose metabolism must be off the scale. Throughout my entire career, I have been able to eat and drink whatever I like and never really put on weight. Even now, after a few months of relaxed living and a diet that would give the hardiest of constitutions gout, I am barely a couple of pounds off my fighting weight. A couple of days on a caffeine diet and I'll be prime Kobe beef once again. But just because I'm not carrying any extra weight doesn't mean that I am actually fit to play 90 minutes.

The lads seem like a decent bunch here, too. I know it's only one day in but there don't seem to be any super-egos, nor does there seem to be any potential conflict of character with anyone, as can sometimes happen when a new player arrives at a club and upsets the established balance. I was my usual polite and forthcoming self, but it may take a little while to see where I fit among the group.

With any team environment, it is important to ascertain where you are positioned within the group. If a place doesn't instantly become clear, then you need to establish it. The worst thing that you can do when you arrive at a new club is to upset the natural order without a basis of merit for doing so, and this merit is gained in different ways. If you're a big-money signing for a club then there is no doubt that the reputation of your ability will go before you, so you don't really need to do anything more. This is quite rare, though, and most players have to find their position in other ways. It can be done with an impressive debut or a high-impact first training session. For some it can be their personality or a fantastic sense of humour which instantly breaks the ice. For others it can be seizing an opportunity to put down a marker, a statement of intent, and that is what I remember doing at QPR back in July 2000.

We had finished the first training session a few days in to my time at Loftus Road, and a couple of players were messing about with a ball, practising tricks and skills. Leon

Jeanne was a young Welsh lad who had phenomenal pace and extremely quick feet; he was being touted as one of the Rs' brightest prospects. Richard Langley alongside him was also being hailed as a future star. An athletic midfielder with a good passing range and a penchant for the spectacular, he was already considered a first-team regular at 20. As I walked over towards the pair, Leon stepped up his little Skill School show and started calling me out.

'Can he stop this, though, Langers?' (double step-over)

'What's he gonna do when I do this, Rich?' (Cruyff turn with drag-back)

Never one to shirk a challenge, I squared Leon up, one v one style, and dared him to try to get past me. He flashed a huge grin that bared his shiny gold tooth and then started towards me. When he got to within a couple of yards, he did three rapid step-overs, dropped his shoulder to my right pushed the ball past my left and went to accelerate past my left shoulder.

Now, Leon's first mistake was to challenge me on my first day. Unbeknown to him, I was going to seize any opportunity to establish myself within this new order. As I've explained, it is mandatory to do this when a new wolf enters the pack, as he must prove himself, and poor Leon was to be my platform. His second mistake was to push down the left-hand side of a right-footed defender. Two things were now in my favour: the fact that I was turning and pushing off my strongest foot in this little duel of ours, and, by going off that foot, I would be turning into Leon with my strongest arm in order to cut off his path to the ball. And cut him off I did, at the neck, with one of the heaviest forearm smashes I've ever hit anyone with. Leon crumpled to the floor while I stepped on to the loose ball and passed it to Langers.

'Oooooooooohhhhhh,' shouted Rich.

'It's a foul, Rich; it's a free-kick, Rich,' wheezed Leon from the turf.

'He just owned you, Leon,' replied Langley, without much sympathy.

And with that comment I strode back to the dressing rooms with the confidence of a man who'd just established his position in the hierarchy.

It can be quite amazing the lengths that some lads will go to when trying to fit in with a group. A couple of days in and I'm not entirely sure what I am going to do here. I'm supposed to be the former Premier League player, the leader, the quality; but I'm unfit, I'm doubting my ability to produce after a period out of the game and I'm not yet sure what the group makes of me.

When I signed for Preston last season, I bowled in there like the big nut, because I felt it. Smiling, cheerful, confident, loud in training and games, I really fancied myself as the top dog. So why don't I feel that here? As silly as it sounds, not driving is part of it, and also what I'm not driving. The white Audi Q7 4.2 pimp mobile that I rocked up to Preston in had a big wow factor. The fact that it was on HP and I was paying through that nose for it was beside the point. It was a status symbol, a visual reminder that I had played at the top level and, as much as we would like to deny it, there is an incredibly materialistic side to the game. You only need to watch any team coming off a coach and you'll see the ubiquitous Beats by Dre headphones and Louis Vuitton washbags. So, to come to York and not only be without that car, but also having to cadge lifts off any- and everyone seriously undermines the impression I'm trying to convey. It's materialistic and superficial, but all part of the reality of being a newbie.

I have seen so many things in my time when it comes to how people try to fit in with the group, and the spectrum of behaviours is huge. Head tennis, darts, snooker and golf are commonplace activities at most clubs and many players will find their social circle there. There are others who go that extra mile to make their mark, though, and whether it's in the name of entertainment, fitting in, or just notoriety, I'll let you be the judge.

There was one player who used to stand and urinate into his own mouth, which was both intriguing and revolting at the same time. Another player used to wet himself in the middle of meetings on the training pitch. It was never funnier than in winter time when steam used to billow off his leg like he was standing in a bonfire. The laughter would soon stop when he then proceeded to jump on other players' backs with piss still flowing down his legs. Another lad used to crap on a length of toilet roll and then take it for 'walkies' down the corridor, whistling as he went and calling, 'Here boy, come on boy.'

The infatuation with faecal matter didn't stop there. One lad would shit in random places. We found it in a boot box, a football boot, on a plate in the fridge, on his side plate at dinner, in his pint on a night out, in the stand-up urinal in the dressing room and floating in the communal bath. These all paled into insignificance when one lad sat at the table in a pub one night asking people for a light. It looked like he had the mother of all cigars between his lips until you looked a little closer . . . Yes, between his lips! A couple of lads at one club took to sending each other pictures of poo coming out mid-flow.

These are rather extreme examples, but there are some clubs where things happen that just wouldn't work anywhere else. The group we had at Burnley was on a different level. If you were coming out of the shower naked, then someone would either try to yank your cock with a shout of 'Give us that a minute', or you would get a full-force slap on the arse, accompanied with the shout 'Get up there'. It was a challenge at first to explain the red cheeks to Mrs C, until it became commonplace.

I don't think any of these would be suitable for me to introduce to a new group, not yet anyway. It's my debut tomorrow, hopefully that can be where I lay my marker down and there'll be no need for any other foolishness.

As debuts go, York City v Oxford United in League 2 isn't the most glamorous of games, but the worries that were going through my head beforehand made me positively nauseous. I was thinking: this game could be a major humiliation for me, as I've been sat on my backside for the best part of three months and I'm going into a competitive league fixture after only two days of training. I could really blow a major gasket here. It would be hugely embarrassing to bow out in this way. But, ever the optimist, I know that I will give it my best. I'm going to have to draw on all of my experience to get through the game. If I manage to position myself so that I never have any straight foot races, I should cope with the fact that I won't have the pace yet. And if I limit the number of set pieces that I go forward for, I won't have to do the draining 50-yard recovery sprint back into position.

However, I knew that my attempts to keep a low profile and be as inconspicuous as possible were not helped by the bastard boots I'd been sent by my agent, Colin Gordon.

Having all but retired in the summer, I hadn't collected any of my boots from Northampton or Burnley at the end of last season, so all I had was a couple of pairs with moulded studs that were in my garage. Having been educated by the 'old school', I had been taught that centre-halves always wear studs. Why? Because you can't hurt strikers with moulds. As archaic as the notion is, it has stuck with me to this day. I don't believe I've ever played a competitive game in moulded studs, and that wasn't going to change now.

I rang Col and asked if he had any boots in the office and he sent me over some beauties: a claret pair of Nike Tiempos. They were stinking. The boys howled when they saw them emerge from the box. I, on the other hand, prayed that they weren't beacons that drew attention to what I was doing. I had already been fined for the trainers I was wearing. Nobody saw fit to warn me that you have to wear white trainers and white socks on match day. I protested my innocence by claiming that I hadn't seen the guidelines, let alone signed a fine sheet, but I calmed down when I realised that the fine was just three pounds. Even I could afford that.

Fines systems at football clubs are generally the same when it comes to what the manager imposes. The club will have a schedule that all players sign up to when they join. They usually scale from ten per cent of a week's wage for minor misdemeanours, rising to two weeks' wages for serious transgressions. Two weeks is actually the maximum that any club can fine a player before it has to be brought to the PFA. I think that it can rise to between six and eight weeks' wages for cases of gross misconduct or breaches of contract, but this has to be ratified by the FA and will usually be mitigated by the union.

In-house fine systems are usually put in place by the

players. All of the money collected is then used to pay for a Christmas or end-of-season party. At the rather more wealthy or conscientious clubs, the funds might be donated to a charity, but you'd be surprised how hard it is to get a whole squad to agree to that. The £3 levy at York is a paltry sum in comparison to other clubs. Even at Preston the base rate was £20. But at the bigger clubs you have to dole out bigger sums and I remember being fined £200 at Leeds for some minor indiscretion, while the top level there was £1000. Needless to say, I kept my nose clean for the entire 15 months.

That was as relaxed as it got for me. The roar of the crowd as we emerged from the tunnel at Bootham Crescent was a far cry from Maine Road in 1998, but it was enough to conjure more nerves and fear than at any other time in my career. 'This is it, Clarke. Let's see if you can still do it,' I told myself.

What ensued was 90 minutes of football that took me to the edge. There were periods in the first half when I could barely see, I was that tired. There is no amount of pre-season training that gets you to the level of fitness required to play that first competitive match of the season. That's after six to eight weeks of intense training specifically designed to get you ready for action. Imagine how I felt after two days of preparation for this.

The second half was an experience I'll never forget. I felt like I was at death's door, my heart was pounding so fast that I thought I was having palpitations. To make things worse, I was touching cloth. At one stage, I hoped well into the half, I asked the ref how long left and he said 27 minutes, plus stoppages. I could've cried. There is nowhere to go when you need the loo on the pitch, absolutely no way out. I was getting stomach cramps in waves. Any pictures from this game will show me grimacing, and that was just from the effort needed to stop me soiling myself.

In actual fact, the distraction that this gave me probably helped me get through the game. I was no longer worried about my fitness or positioning, everything was done on auto-pilot. The relief I experienced at the final whistle was multi-layered, let me tell you. The Royal Doulton took a bashing, but so did my doubts. We won the tie 3-1 and it felt magnificent. I had used all my knowledge to get through this match. I had tentatively come back to football and she had taken me by the hand once more. You are damn right I can do this and, do you know what?

I fucking love football!

Showering afterwards, there was a little buzz of excitement in the air. It was only when I realised that it was because there were two new urinals in the dressing room that the change in circumstance hit home. I bet Giggs and Scholes have never high-fived because they'd had a toilet fitted.

Saying that, when Burnley got promoted to the Premier League, I remember that we were incredibly excited about having two new showers fitted in the dressing room, doubling the capacity and meaning that we wouldn't need to use the big communal bath as much. I say that like the communal bath is a bad thing. It's awesome. I first experienced it at Blackpool. We had one at both the stadium and the training ground. The hygiene levels were off the charts, though. As YTs we couldn't use it until after all of the first team had finished, and there was never enough hot water to run a fresh one. This resulted in us bathing alongside black, brown and ginger spiders' legs in water that was distinctly yellow. We'd have been better off bathing in the sea, even at Blackpool.

CHAPTER 6

ON THE PHYSIO'S COUCH

There are a few things that are certain in the world of football: Man Utd will get a winner in the ninth minute of injury time at Old Trafford, England will lose on penalties and, at some point in their career, a player will get injured. After throwing myself into a league game only 48 hours after my first training session of the season, I expected my muscles to be screaming at me in submission, but they were holding up better than expected. Barring the typical post-match soreness my body was faring pretty well with the sudden level of exertion. I didn't have too long to wait for my first sessions in the York City physio's room, though.

My debut was quickly followed by a Johnstone's Paint Trophy tie away at Rotherham on the Tuesday. They have a lovely new stadium there at the Don Valley; it's a bit flat-packed, like a lot of the new developments, but more than adequate for what a club such as Rotherham needs. It's a million miles from the athletics track they were playing in a few years before.

My second game in just over three days is going to tell me a lot about myself, both physically and mentally. How soon my body fails will show me how far behind the rest of the squad I am, but it is relatively immaterial. I know that I will get fitter as I get more games under my belt. How my head reacts to my body capitulating is of far greater significance. There will come a time in this game when I will hit the brick wall: my lungs will feel like unstretched water balloons, so constricted that no air can get in; my legs will feel like they weigh 18 stone apiece and my feet will be nailed to the floor. It happens to all players at some point, but your mind gets you through. Whatever your motivation is – money, bonuses, kudos, victory, trophies, headlines, pride – it doesn't matter, it drives you past this point of pain. However, I'm a tad concerned that I may get a dose of the 'Bardsleys' when I reach the stage that I feel I can't go on. Will the questions that meandered around my mind in the summer rush through like the waters of Niagara, or will this new-found realisation that I still love the game carry me through?

I needn't have worried. Just as in the Oxford game, a distraction befell me that meant I rarely thought about my cardiovascular fitness. About 20 minutes into the game, I went up for a header and landed awkwardly on my right leg, rocking my ankle. I hobbled around for a few minutes but then carried on like a warrior. Having just scraped my way back into a team, I wasn't going to let it go easily. We won the game 1-0 and I managed to grind out the full 90 minutes. Sitting down in the dressing room, I knew that I was in for a rough night once I took the strapping off my ankle.

I have melodramatic ankles at the best of times, due to having injured them on so many occasions. It takes only a minor knock and they swell up like I have elephantiasis. Once the swelling goes down, there is usually little or no actual damage to the joint structures. Knowing this enables me to make an executive decision when incidents like this occur. After a few minutes hobbling up and down the touchline, I can tell if it's serious or not. I probably won't be able to train for the next couple of days, but that is just because of the fluid in there. If I ice it, rest it and then strap it up at the weekend, I should be able get out on the pitch again. I hate physio rooms, too. They just reek of negativity. It is very hard being injured, because you instantly fall outside of the group. Suddenly you are of no use to the manager, and you're a burden to your physio and falling short of your own dreams and goals. It is not a nice place to be. I would rather train at 60 per cent fit than spend time in there, so I'm going to keep this one as brief as possible.

Two weeks and two draws later, we travelled to Burton for a league fixture. This was my fifth game in 18 days and I have been delighted with my levels of fitness and performance. Having narrowly avoided a lengthy lay-off due to my ankle injury, and being unbeaten in the first four games, I was feeling pretty confident. Half an hour in, the big clumsy oaf that is Calvin Zola caught me in an attempt to latch on to a through ball that I was shepherding back to the keeper. I knew instantly that I couldn't perform the same warhorse-like effort as I had done at Rotherham.

There was a shooting pain through my Achilles that made it feel like it would give way with every step. As I tried in vain to 'shake it off', refusing assistance to get off the pitch in the hope that the next footstep would provide a miraculous recovery, I was blissfully unaware that I was giving my team-mates a moment of hilarity. Instead of expressing concern about my plight, I was informed the next day how the boys in the stand were in creases at my spasmodic exit. Apparently it looked like I was walking on the live rail, getting electric shocks with every step, shaking like my left leg was made of jelly and my right was a pneumatic drill. Meanwhile our physio kept cool and was strolling alongside me like it was a daily occurrence.

In a way, I'm glad that I wasn't stretchered off. I think it's wholly unnecessary unless you have done serious damage. Some of the broken fingernails and dislodged hairdos that have required 'treatment' are just beyond a joke. It must be tough for a referee to judge whether a player has a serious injury or if he's just over-egging a minor knock. After the terrible incident with Fabrice Muamba, I think all players should make every effort to minimise the dramatics that come with their response to tackles and possible injuries. Those precious moments while the referee is deciding if you genuinely need assistance or not could be the difference between life and death. The number of life-threatening incidents may be few and far between, but being on the wrong side of even one decision of this magnitude would be utterly tragic, and we would all have had a part to play.

I didn't find it funny that evening. Describing the pain that swollen joints give at night is almost impossible. All of your other senses heighten when it's dark and you close your eyes. Your hearing becomes more acute, as does your sense of touch. You'll be familiar with the dripping tap that can be heard from three miles away, along with the minuscule crumb on your bed sheet that is impossible to brush away. Factor the increase in awareness of these small things into something that is already pulsing with pain under normal circumstances: it is all-consuming, especially when you have a compression bandage on the ankle, squeezing the living daylights out of your foot and increasing the sensitivity of the joint.

The first night of an ankle injury I will be lucky to get an hour's sleep. I usually end up tearing the strapping off at around four or five in the morning because it has started to cause a burning sensation and the immediate relief is beautiful. For seven seconds. Then the blood flow returns to the joint like a tsunami and you remember why you had the strapping on in the first place. It happens so often now, though, that Mrs C doesn't even bother to wake up and ask if I'm all right. I remember way back when she used to see if she could get me anything, and she would bring painkillers to me and stroke my head. Now she sleeps. There is nothing to be done about it. She knows it, and I know it, so there's no point in both of us not getting a night's sleep.

This little episode is barely a footnote in the 'Injuries' section of my career. I've picked up some varied and strange ones along the way. I remember big Emile Heskey breaking my toe at Villa Park. Somehow this went undetected despite my having three x-rays, but I was insistent that it was broken. The pain in it was constant and, at times, unbearable. However, after the third opinion, I even started to doubt myself. I just might have accepted it if my toe hadn't resembled a genetically modified chipolata. When Chris Eagles taped a brown two-litre bottle of pop to his middle toe and strolled into the dressing room to howls of laughter from my team-mates, I knew it wasn't normal.

It was after this incident that I realised how little credence is often given to a player's thoughts about his own body. Granted, we have qualified physios and medical professionals on hand to diagnose and assess our ailments, and we should respect their opinions, but surely no one knows their own body better than the person concerned? I played four matches through this period and, because we'd been told there wasn't anything wrong, I was having painkilling injections in my foot before each game. These jabs were meant to last between four and six hours. Alarm bells should have probably started ringing when I needed another set of jabs at half time to get me through the next 45 minutes. But no, apparently I was just being soft.

Another strange injury was one that robbed me of a play-off final at the Millennium Stadium and the majority of the Premier League season that subsequently followed. I tore my rectus femoris, or hip flexor, and missed the entire play-off section of our promotion with Watford in 2006. I am actually quite glad that this happened. I know that's a strange thing to say, but if I hadn't been injured then I would have been deprived of a play-off final place in any case. The reason was that when I transferred from Leeds United to Watford, chairman Ken Bates and manager Kevin Blackwell made it a sticking point that I couldn't go unless I agreed not to play against Leeds that season. This is something that often happens with loan moves, and rightly so as there is an obvious conflict of interests. In permanent transfers, though, it is pretty much unheard of, and these two were seemingly playing silly buggers. Surely it is a restriction of trade? I suppose it compares to 'non-compete' clauses that you see in the business world. But it did mean one thing: when Leeds played Preston in the semi-final, I had never wanted Preston to win so much in all my life. I had a chance of being fit for the final and I didn't want that to be taken from me because of some strange clause in my contract.

As it happened, it was immaterial. My hip flexor kept breaking down. I would get about four or five weeks into rehabilitation, being able to do all the tests laid out before me, and then 'pop', there it goes again. Andy Rolls is one of the best physios I have had in my time. He knows his stuff, but he's also willing to listen at the same time. He's a compassionate physio, which is quite rare. When I broke down for the third time – which, annoyingly, was during pre-season for our assault on the Premier League – Rollsy knew something wasn't quite right.

Muscle injuries are usually scanned using MRI, which gives a detailed picture of the muscles, tendons and ligaments in a selected area, but not the bone. I had had three already and they all showed the same thing: a minor injury that should have healed in four to six weeks. Nobody thought to x-ray my leg because it wasn't a bone injury. But Andy suggested we went to see a specialist in central London, and he asked if I'd had an x-ray, which obviously I hadn't. It seemed rather strange to x-ray a muscle, but we did so nonetheless, and am I glad we did.

Instead of forming scar tissue in the muscle injury, my body had been making bone tissue. This meant that I had three small pieces of bone in my muscle that were impeding me. Any time I called for maximal exertion, the muscle would effectively short-circuit because of the foreign bodies in there, causing me to break down. I was delighted to finally have the answer to my injury riddle, but I was devastated when I found out what the treatment was. I had to do nothing for three months and take pills to de-calcify my body. I wasn't allowed to do anything because while the pills would break down the little intruders in my thigh they also made my bones brittle.

Once the course of pills was finished, I had to get my leg x-rayed again to check the bone fragments were gone, and then I had to re-calcify my body. This process was equally as long, because there is only so much calcium your body can take on board at any given time. As my bones got stronger, I could increase my workload progressively and I managed to return to the first team after a loan spell at Luton.

I finally became a Premier League player on 9 April 2007, Watford v Portsmouth, and we won 4-2. It was an awesome moment. It was a baking hot day at Vicarage Road, I had freshly shaved my head and I was ready for this. All of my life I had wanted to be a top-flight player and now it was coming true. The game flew by as if I were watching a Grand Prix.

I can remember only one thing from the match: it was the moment I made possibly the best tackle of my career. The ball was played up to Lomana Tresor LuaLua on the halfway line, as he pulled ten yards off in front of our defensive line. I was sprinting towards him so that he couldn't turn into open space. As I approached, I noticed that he was opening his body out as though he was going let the ball run across him where it would come straight to me. I also realised that he hadn't once looked behind him. 'He doesn't know I'm coming,' I thought as I closed the gap between us.

I was now going full speed and all the time assessing if he knew I was there. There was every chance that he was faking the movement in order to entice a big, dumb centre-half like me into a tackle, so that he could use some sublime Premier League skill and leave me standing. He'd done it to me before at Loftus Road and I hadn't forgotten it, but I knew that if he didn't look in the next two yards, he would get it. And so he did. As he took his first touch on the half-turn, I already had a full boot on the ball. While he was processing where on earth I had appeared from, my momentum took me clean through him and he got a bit of hang time. I'm not sure what was louder, the sound of the tackle or the sound of him hitting the floor three seconds later. It was a beauty. It would probably be a standard red card nowadays, but it was deemed a fantastic challenge back then.

If that injury at least had a happy ending, my worst one very nearly didn't.

— CHAPTER 7 —

A CAN OF CARLING AND 56 LITTLE FRIENDS

The mother of all injuries in my career was one that would take me to possibly the darkest moment of my life. I had just embarked on my big move from Blackpool down to Queens Park Rangers. The contrast between the two clubs at that time was huge. Blackpool had just been relegated to Division 3 after the 1999-00 season and QPR were in Division 1. QPR's training ground in Acton wasn't spectacular, but at least it was a permanent building and not something that resembled a garden shed. The grounds were like chalk and cheese. Bloomfield Road was crumbling, weather-beaten, with a condemned kop; whereas Loftus Road was all-seater, all-covered, shiny yet intimate.

Blackpool has a busy summer season, but that's nothing compared to the 24/7 hustle and bustle of the Smoke. The increase in my wages meant that I felt like a millionaire by comparison with the grind of the first 20 years of my life, and now I could enjoy my new-found wealth in the complete anonymity of West London. I was leaving the bright lights of Blackpool Illuminations and the intense scrutiny of a small-town club to come and revel in the invisibility that the capital gives a six-foot mixed-race man. It was awesome.

On the pitch I had made a great start at Rangers. It can sometimes take a while for players to settle at a new club, especially if it is a bigger club than their previous one. But making a move like this suited my character to a T. I have always endeavoured to prove myself at whatever I've done or whichever club I've joined. Giving myself that burden of expectation means that I *have* to succeed. Having to make enough of an impact to replace experienced internationals such as Steve Morrow and Karl Ready in the team was exactly what I needed, because it brought the best out of me.

I had made the starting line-up for the first game of the season, a home match against Birmingham City, where I had a memorable tussle with Geoff Horsfield. Defences came out on top on a blazing August Saturday afternoon in a 0-0 draw, and it was my debut performance that stole the headlines (I still have the paper cuttings to prove it!). Only three games into my QPR career, I earned my first international call-up, for England Under-21s. This was such a significant moment in my life. The feelings of pride, excitement and disbelief danced a fandango around my brain as I tried to process this meteoric rise. I donned the Three Lions shirt at Middlesbrough for a friendly against Georgia in what was then called the BT Cellnet Riverside Stadium.

Four years earlier, my parents and grandfather had been in the stand to witness me scoring my first-ever professional goal and that brought us all to tears. Just imagine what this moment did for us. I gave my first cap to my granddad, a man who has supported and followed my football for my entire life. I don't think there was a better thank-you that I could offer in return for all his dedication. His support was only surpassed by my parents, especially my dad, to whom I gave my first England shirt, which I signed with a little poem of gratitude.

To me personally, this was the most significant indication that I had finally 'made it'. Just four or five months beforehand, I had been watching *Match of the Day* with the same hopes and dreams that I had had at 11 years of age. I watched those footballers playing in fantastic stadiums for clubs that are renowned the world over, and I wanted to be just like them.

I had been watching Ashley Cole emerge as Arsenal's new generation of full-back, David Dunn become the 'local boy done good' at Blackburn, Darius Vassell break through the ranks at Villa, Joe Cole and Michael Carrick dominate the midfield at West Ham, and Paul Robinson bring young blood into an old man's position. Now I was sat playing cards with them at the back of the team bus. Not only was I taken aback to be in the same team as these guys, but they were playing cards for stakes that were off the scale. Shoot pontoon is the devil's game, and hundreds of pounds were being thrown into the pot with every hand. Paulo Vernazza won a few grand one trip, more than I earned in a week, even on my new mega-money deal. This was a whole new level and I liked it.

Back at club level, we had signed Peter Crouch from Tottenham. He is without doubt the most skilful tall footballer I have ever seen, even to this day. His tricks with the ball were phenomenal and he was even very strong in the air, which is rarer than you might think for tall young lads, especially when they come through elite academies.

Crouchy is great banter, especially on a night out. I've never seen such tekkers on the dancefloor for a big guy. I vaguely remember going to a pub in Ealing on Christmas Eve with him. It was absolutely heaving and he was a legend in there, high-fiving people, just like Roy Munson from *Kingpin*. Drinks flowed and laughter rang out long into the night. Even though we were having a tough time on the pitch, this new world that was opened up to me, one of fame, status and celebrity, was exhilarating. I was rubbing shoulders with the big boys. I may not have been eating at the same table as the king, but the crumbs off it were a feast in themselves.

My performances at club level were gaining praise from many quarters as I revelled in the 5-3-2 formation that Gerry Francis preferred. I was able to play as a marauding centre-half, overlapping my wing-back and getting crosses in the box. I was truly loving life.

It was 31 January 2001 and a bitterly cold night in Shepherd's Bush. The match against Fulham was a West London derby and tensions were running high. Fulham were cruising at the top of the league and heading for the Premier League while we were struggling for form and slipping towards the bottom. Gerry had let us know in no uncertain terms that there was a huge amount of pressure on him, and therefore us, to get a result.

At 1-0 down in the first half, I went in for a seemingly innocuous challenge with Rufus Brevett in the centre circle. We raced to reach a loose ball and seemed destined for a head-on collision. As I went to strike the ball he managed to toe-poke it away and we collapsed in a heap on the floor. We untangled our limbs and Rufus got up and strode away, but as I tried to get to my feet I knew something was very wrong. There wasn't any excruciating pain or audible snap, but I had a sensation that my leg was in an unnatural position.

I am the type of player that instantly tries to get up and run off an injury, never letting an opponent know that they've hurt you, but this time my brain told me not to move. Bob Oteng, the kit man, came on to assess the extent of my 'knock' and quickly saw that I couldn't continue. It was the second time in my career that I had to be stretchered off the pitch, and the reaction of the crowd, a round of warm applause, was in stark contrast to that of the manager. There was no river of blood or visible break, no cartoon-like swelling on my leg to show him that this was a legitimate injury. The incident had appeared to be a relatively minor one. Perhaps it wasn't surprising that he gave me a disgusted look as I was carried past and, after the game, he made a flippant remark along the lines of 'it had better be something serious'.

It was. When I was given the diagnosis by my knee specialist, Mr Andy Williams, he told me I had ruptured my anterior cruciate ligament (ACL), lateral collateral ligament (LCL), popliteus ligament, snapped the ilio tibial band (ITB – which is supposed to have the tensile strength of steel), torn one of the heads of my biceps femoris muscle from the bone and rotated the fibula head, which in turn dislodged the nerve. In short, my knee was fucked. To add insult to injury, there was no way of assessing the extent of the damage to the nerve during its displacement. It would only be post-op that we would know whether I had sustained a 'floppy foot', like Gigi Casiraghi at Chelsea. Andy couldn't even guarantee that I would be able to walk unaided again, let alone get back to playing football. In short, a few months after my 21st birthday, I was facing the prospect of the end of my career.

The news hit me like a train. I was just emerging on to the football scene, and beginning to show the world what I was capable of. Not only that, my performances had been recognised, as I'd played in the first three England Under-21 games of the season. What the hell would I do now? Football was all I'd ever known. At that point in my life, it was my reason to get out of bed in the morning and still formed most of the dreams that entertained me in my sleep. It was my life.

I sat down with Brian and his assistant physio Prav Mathema the following day to discuss my next steps. They didn't know what to say. In truth, there wasn't anything they could say. I had to get booked in for an operation and then, well, the rest was in the lap of the gods. I was utterly devoid of thought. I think it was my body's way of protecting itself. I didn't rant and rage at the injustice of it all; I didn't cry and scream at the terrifying thought of this being the end of my career; I just sat there, vacant and glazed, while Brian tried to talk me through what would happen next.

His words drifted past my ears like some distant whisper, not registering, not making any real sense, as I gazed out of the window at the lads training on the pitch. 'You lucky bastards,' I thought. I was brought back into the room by the feel of Brian patting me on the shoulder. 'Take a few days off,' he suggested. 'Get your head together.' That sounded like a good idea to me, and we both must have thought exactly the same thing, because he turned to me as

I walked out the door and said: 'You might as well have a few pints.'

It's the universal response in times of trauma, to go and have a drink, so drink I did. I had a few nights out in the week before my operation, but the really heavy drinking started post-op. I was pretty much housebound for the first few weeks after the operation, save for an hour or so every couple of days in the treatment room. Being on crutches with my knee in a brace didn't hold me back one iota. When I was in the house the pain was excruciating, even with the strongest painkillers that the doc could prescribe, co-proxamol I think they were called. What was a much better anaesthetic was alcohol, the juice of Zeus. I would get smashed virtually every day. When the pain was too much for me to make it out of my flat in Acton, I would call Dial-a-Crate, an amazing company that would deliver a crate of Carling, two bottles of Chablis and 40 Marlboro Lights to my door, any time of day. I didn't even have to move.

As I slowly pickled my body, my brain was attempting to evaluate my predicament in sporadic moments of rational thought. I was in London, more than 200 miles from my family in Preston. I had walked out on my fiancée when I moved to QPR. It was a relationship I didn't want to be in, but in doing so I had virtually abandoned my 18-month-old daughter. Yes, I was supporting them financially, but in my own mind I had all but absolved myself of any responsibility towards her as a father.

Instead, I was living in a sparsely decorated two-bed flat above a pub in Acton which, although in the centre of a town, was very lonely indeed. When I had been seeing this set-up as the beginning of a burgeoning career in football, it was all worth it to me. I would walk over hot coals for football, sacrificing anything and everything if I had to, so all of this was part of an exciting journey. The end justified the means. But when the end had apparently been taken away from me, then what the hell did I have left? Football defined me at this point, and without it I had nothing, I was nothing. I had actually started a new relationship with an Ealing girl called Racheal (yes, spelt like that), but even the early blossoms of young love could not sway me from this train of thought.

When I wasn't sitting in my flat working my way through the Dial-a-Crate, I was spending more and more time in the bookie's across the road, back in the days when you could smoke in there, lining up with the grey-haired old men and their roll-up ciggies. I had never been one for the gee-gees, but I didn't mind having a punt on the dogs. I also spent hours on the fruit machines, something that I had become obsessed with while I was at Blackpool, where the amusement arcades kept on drawing me in. The difference now was that I was losing hundreds, if not thousands, at a time instead of tens and twenties.

One weekend it all came to a head. I had polished off my Dial-a-Crate delivery the day before, so was feeling those post-alcohol blues that some of you may be familiar with. I like to call them the wardrobe monsters.

'What did you do last night?'

'Oh my God, they are going to HATE you.'

'You absolute fool, what on earth did you do that for?'

'What the hell are you going to say or do about this?'

I had blown all my money and had no football. These were the things that meant everything to me at the time.

Without money I couldn't make any friends and without football I couldn't make anyone proud. I was making no visible progress with my injury and I could not see any kind of future. I wanted out.

I gathered all of the co-proxamol that I had in the flat and hobbled down to the park at the bottom of my road. I sat on a swing for about 20 minutes. As I sat there, I wondered who would miss me. My warped mindset meant that I found reasons for most people to want me to do it. I thought Racheal might miss me, but she'd get over it, as we'd not been together long. I knew my granddad would be upset too, but thought that as he had loads of other grandchildren he'd be okay.

Just do it.

So I popped 56 tablets out of their foil wrapper and swallowed them, handful by handful, with a can of Carling. I hope this doesn't sound perverse, but at this point I was a little bit excited. I wasn't sure what was going to happen. I wondered if I might have some kind of cinematic death scene where my body exploded, or I started to convulse and froth at the mouth. What if I passed out and collapsed in the middle of the park?

I sat on the swing for a few more minutes and finished my beer. Nothing seemed to be happening. What a letdown, a real anticlimax. I couldn't even top myself properly. So I hobbled back up to the flat and got into bed. Racheal came around, quite unexpectedly, and instantly she knew something was wrong. I don't know how, or why, but she just kept asking me what was wrong, over and over.

'Nothing,' I replied. 'Let's just go to sleep.'

I remember thinking that if I could just get to sleep then

I might never have to wake up. I could die in my sleep – beautiful. But she just would not let me lie down.

The next moments are really rather hazy. I couldn't tell you if I was taken to hospital by Racheal or in an ambulance, but the next clear memory I have is of being in a hospital bed and a doctor or nurse asking me if I want my stomach pumped. I refused, continually. The next thing I remember is Racheal's dad John appearing in my vision. I don't know if he convinced me to allow them to do it, or if he just took a kind of 'power of attorney', but almost instantly I had a tube put down my throat and all sorts of people seemed to be rushing about. It all gets hazy again after that, but I know that he and Racheal saved my life.

I had to see the hospital psychiatrist the next day before I could be discharged. We went through a vague chat about the reasons I'd tried to kill myself, and then I was told I could go as long as I agreed to make another appointment with them.

It transpired that they pumped 52 whole co-proxamol out of my stomach, some six or seven hours after I'd taken them. There were just four partially digested ones. They couldn't explain how that had happened, or why. I was told that I may have sustained some liver damage, but they wouldn't be able to assess that until any subsequent symptoms displayed themselves.

Racheal took me back to her house, where I stayed with her family for a few days. I went back to work and carried on with my rehab as normal. Prav pulled me to one side and told me that he was there if I ever needed anyone to talk to, and that if I was ever feeling like that again I should come to him. I really appreciated his kindness and support, but this was something that I wanted to quickly forget, as did everyone else, and so we did.

It has taken me about four weeks to write about this incident. I have been putting it off repeatedly because I've never been back there before. Even in all my counselling, in all the conversations I've had with family, friends and my wife, this is still just 'something that happened to me once' and I've never fully assessed why. There are so many feelings surrounding this that I have not wanted to face.

There is guilt. I feel guilty that I had virtually abandoned my daughter at the time. I had run away from my responsibilities as a father with an 'out of sight, out of mind' attitude. In trying to do this, I hadn't even contemplated the repercussions for her. I had put football ahead of her, and I had put my own lifestyle ahead of her, too. I feel guilty that my values were so materialistic, that I didn't recognise the value of family, of parenthood, and of loving relationships. I feel guilty that I put Racheal and her family through that ordeal at close quarters, without the balls to talk about it with them afterwards, or ever to tell them how truly grateful I am for what they did for me. Basically, I was a coward. I didn't want to have to face my problems. I didn't have the wherewithal to face my responsibilities. From my warped and clouded viewpoint, all I could see was myself.

Along with guilt there is shame, lots of shame. I thought that the best way to deal with my problems was to run away from them. It seemed the easiest way, at least. It's a typical addict's mindset. Whatever I did or wherever I went to get away from these problems, there was always one constant: me! It took me many years to realise that fact. I guess it's something I will spend my whole life keeping on learning.

CHAPTER 8

YOU'RE SHIT AND YOU KNOW YOU ARE

F ortunately I'm not in such a bad place with this injury I have now. Even so, when you are injured you get to experience a match from a completely different perspective. Every club that I have been at expects all injured players to report to the stadium on match day and to support the team, which is completely understandable. This can be tough for a player, though, especially if he is a long-term casualty. The match is the focal point of your week, your season, your life. It is the very thing that you have always been preparing for, what you made sacrifices for as a kid, teenager and now as an adult. It is the very thing that gives the whole industry of football a purpose.

When the match-day game is taken away from you for no reason of your own doing, it feels like a total injustice. When you are then forced to come and watch the very occasion that gives your life some kind of definition, and observe some other guy profiting from your misfortune, it feels like a warped form of mental torture. You watch with twisted thinking, wanting the team to do well, but not *that* well. As a defender, if I'm on the sidelines I want the team to win

7-6, but there's always a part of me that wants my replacement to have an absolute nightmare, maybe scoring two own goals. It sounds crazy but it's true, and any player who tells you different is almost certainly lying.

The insecurity of not being on the pitch is all-consuming: 'Will I get straight back in the team? Will my replacement have a blinder and keep me on the sidelines when I'm fit? Will the gaffer bring in reinforcements, creating even further competition for my place?'

You can almost see these thought bubbles coming out of the heads of injured and unselected players when they are loitering around the dressing room. For this reason, many managers keep non-squad players away from the group on a match day, because they don't want the negativity to be infectious. The protocol here at York is much like the vast majority of clubs. All players report to the dressing room an hour and 45 minutes before kick-off, and then non-squad players vacate the room after the team meeting, somewhere between 60 and 75 minutes before the game. We give our best wishes to the players, with sincerity in most cases, but not for *that* guy. We want him to have the mother of all stinkers, but we still shake his hand anyway. We're then banished from sight, bumbling around the ground until the main event when we take our seats in the stand.

It is here that we get to observe things from a new angle, not just the game but the action in the stands, too. I need to be very careful with what I say here, but some of the tripe that emanates from the crowd is laughable. I have just sat through a 0-0 draw between York and Cheltenham, which I had to watch from the stands due to my ankle injury. It was one of the most one-sided draws I have ever seen. York dominated from start to finish and, save for one counter-attack where Cheltenham hit the bar with a mis-kick, a 3-0 scoreline would have probably been a fair result.

So what is it that has made this noteworthy enough to warrant a mention here? It was the shouts, groans and utterances from the crowd, including from the chairman! There was nothing more that this team could have done other than score. They ran, harried and hassled, tackled, headed and passed Cheltenham off the park, but when a pass was anything other than pinpoint accurate, the moans were unbelievable. What astonishes me about this response is that this is York, a side that has just come out of the Conference and is making its way up Football League 2, a division notorious for the 'hoofball' that the majority of teams play. This is not Manchester City in the Champions League.

Our lads were playing outstanding one- and two-touch passing football, and Ashley Chambers tried an intricate through ball that would have graced the Premier League. Their defender stuck a hopeful leg out behind him and managed to intercept the pass and nudge it to safety. Instead of applauding the vision, confidence and creativity he'd just seen, the chairman shouted 'look interested' at the top of his voice.

It struck me as a ridiculous comment, but his criticism proved infectious to those around him. I was sitting at the back of the stand with the other non-squad players and we couldn't believe what we were hearing from our fans. It strikes me that such comments come from one of only two places. Either the match is of huge importance and the desire to win is creating feelings of anxiety and frustration, or there is complete ignorance of what is being played out before them. Now, I don't know the chairman well enough yet to make a calculated judgement, but this was a league game in September when the side were sitting just outside the play-offs, so I can only assume it's the latter option.

This leads me on to the relationship between fans and players. Sitting in the stand, the game of football is so easy. The viewing angle means that the whole of the pitch can be seen and analysed from the comfort of your seat. Therefore all potential passes and runs are blatantly obvious to the person sat on their backside munching on a balti pie. The ability to see, appreciate and execute these things at pitch level is what differentiates an average player from a great player, and I sometimes think that this is lost on a lot of fans.

This was exemplified when I was on the train back home from the game. A couple of lads struck up a conversation with me while we stood in the aisle of the packed chugger from York to Manchester. It is quite a regular occurrence that I get recognised on public transport, and I am generally very amenable to those who want to converse, quiz or just ridicule me. It is quite a massaging of the old ego when this occurs, especially when other people notice the interest. You can see them wondering what is going on, and who is the guy whose photo they seem to want.

The two fellas I met on the train tonight were Manchester United fans. They went through the whole rigmarole of deconstructing the industry, pontificating about the lack of social responsibility from the modern-day footballer and how they would change it. They then moved on to players' wages and how immoral they were, stating that it was wrong for Robbie Savage to have earned so much money from football when he's crap. My face must have conveyed my thoughts because they instantly asked what I thought.

The honest answer is that I find it ludicrous that a guy on a train can give a summary judgement on the talents of a man who has had a 20-year career in football. During that career, he amassed 537 league appearances, most of them in the Premier League, he won the League Cup with Leicester City, helped in several promotions and won 39 international caps, but yet he was instantly dismissed. When I explained as much, they dumbfounded me with the cherry of all comments: 'Yeah, but Wales doesn't count, does it?'

There is a complete lack of appreciation from most fans of what it takes to become a professional footballer, and what you have to give up to reach that goal. When you have achieved it, it then takes more effort to be a successful one, and even more again to be an international. I would chop off a finger to play for Wales as many times as Robbie Savage. And whose scale were these guys using to judge him? I wish I had half the ability he has, and a tenth of the success.

I think a lot of people fail to look at what happens beyond the Premier League. They seem to believe that if you are a footballer then you must be a millionaire, earning at least £10,000 per week (if not considerably more), and that a Ferrari sits in your garage alongside a baby Bentley for the missus. At the same time as believing that, some fans also appear to think that if you don't play for Manchester United, City or Chelsea then you must be crap. In fact, the pyramid of talent drifts gently down to the bottom of League 2 (and beyond), but the disparity in income between the leagues is huge – much greater than the disparity in levels of ability. If that weren't the case, a lower league side would never beat a Premier League side in a cup game.

It's probably fortunate that I don't mind arguing the toss

over these issues. My grounding in PFA business gives me so much ammo to fire at narrow-minded views that it is quite enjoyable to discuss these things. Other players aren't always so accommodating. This is usually where the stories of rude, obnoxious players come from. They either have an inability to argue their point or just take umbrage with a person assassinating their character/profession and react with vitriol.

I completely understand this response. There are times when I get fed up with having to justify the viability and validity of football as a profession. It is almost as though the concept of supply and demand shouldn't apply to the game. Why do the best footballers get paid so much? Because football is a multi-billion-pound industry and they are the purveyors of the product. Nobody asks why actors are paid so much, or pop stars, and there are rarely calls for them to fulfil their social responsibilities. If a musician trashes a hotel room, or parties all night, they're 'wild' or 'iconic'. If a footballer does the same they are 'hoodlums'.

I think this is for two reasons. Firstly, there is an illusion of ownership when it comes to football. When I listen to the phone-ins on the radio or talk to some fans, the same points come out again and again:

'We pay your wages.'

'This is our club.'

'There's no loyalty from these mercenaries.'

Utter tripe. Everybody pays everybody else's wages in the world. When I buy a stamp I am paying my postman's wages. When I do my shopping at Tesco, I am paying the shop assistant's wages. When I pay my gas bill, I am paying the rigger's wages. This doesn't mean that I own them; it doesn't give me the right to openly and audibly critique how messy the shelves are to the person's face, or to encourage all the other shoppers to chant that they're a useless wanker. It doesn't give me the right to scream at my postie down the street because my mail is folded or wet. Why should footballers have to put up with this type of abuse?

Now don't get me wrong, the fans' support of the club is very much appreciated, it is in fact vital for the club's existence, but so is the continued business of any customer to any industry. If Sainsbury's were to offer 20 per cent off the price of their groceries, it's highly likely that I would go and shop there.

Last year, my bank manager left to go to another bank because they offered him more money for the same role. If I had then launched a diatribe on Twitter about him, there would have been serious repercussions – for me. The logic of football is not wired that way, though. It is seen as treacherous to leave a club, a betrayal of the support that the fans have given to you. But this is my job; this is what feeds my children. A professional footballer has (on average) eight years to make a lifetime's earnings. In 20 years' time, when you have long forgotten about me and what I gave to the club, I will still have bills to pay and a family to support. Therefore, if I get offered more money for the same role by someone else, of course I am going to seriously consider it. It is not mercenary; it is employment.

The second reason is that football is so tangible for everyone. The vast majority of fans played football as kids, and many still do. Everybody knows somebody who coulda, shoulda, woulda made it if it wasn't for something that prevented them from doing so. It seems as though everybody has had trials at one stage, or feels like they had a chance. Because so many people feel they came so close, I think this lowers the perception of the level of ability required to make it.

It's different in other areas. Everyone can appreciate good singers because we all realise how difficult it is to sing well. When acknowledging a flawless recital or musical performance, no one recalls how they once played a correct note when playing a trombone. They can tell you in minute detail, however, about the volley they once scored in a kick-about on the park when they were 12 years old. There is something about football that is intoxicating. It consumes you, and you can never be released from its grip. That's why fans come back week after week, why thousands of people sit around a TV on a Saturday afternoon watching people sit around a TV watching football. It's insane. Could you imagine watching a programme where a group of people were watching *EastEnders* on a little monitor and they were relaying scenes to you in their own words? It is almost as ludicrous as Alan Partridge's Monkey Tennis.

This is not to say that all interaction between the stands and the pitch is negative; far from it, in fact. I experienced other scenarios over the course of the year that were far more enjoyable, if not strictly respectful. It is commonly stated by footballers that they blank out any shouts or chants from the supporters when the game is in full flow and the majority of the time this is true.

There are circumstances, though, where your awareness of the verbals coming from the perimeter is very much heightened. This is usually when a player is having what is colloquially known as 'a Reggie Blinker'. If you are constantly giving the ball away or missing the target with shots, the pressure starts to mount. The audible groans and jeers that come from the terraces have a huge impact on your concentration. It makes the next thing that you do of paramount importance – you must get it right. This leads to tightening of the muscles and hesitation in decision-making, which almost invariably means that the next thing you do goes wrong as well. On the odd occasion when you actually do something successfully in one of these periods, instead of rebuilding your confidence the ironic cheers from the fans just serve to further bury it. It takes an unbelievably hardened character not to be affected by the audible appraisals that occur during a game.

Another situation where players can't avoid the banter is at some of the more intimate grounds, such as Loftus Road, where the stands are only three or four feet away from the pitch, or when a match has a very low attendance and all shouts reverberate around the entire ground. At times like these, there is no way of escaping from the forked tongue of the over-exuberant, and often inebriated, fan. As much as I want to blank it out because I'm on the pitch, I do laugh, chuckle, frown or recoil when the tirades or witty comments come forth. Over the years I have developed the ability to actually engage with the supporters, both during and after games, as I like to enjoy the *craic* just as much as the next guy. In my mind, however, even if fans are being critical, I think there should be humour and enjoyment behind it all.

While at Preston we had a pre-season match against Blackburn Rovers which was played at the Lancashire County FA headquarters in my hometown of Leyland. There were plenty of familiar faces around the edge of the pitch, including some old school friends who were lifelong PNE supporters. It is always tough to shake off your past in football, and the fact that I had played for the Tangerine Scum up the M55 (Blackpool) *and* the Dingles (Burnley) wasn't going to be passed over whether I was a local lad or not.

We had just won a corner so I sauntered up to join the strikers in the box. The ball came in and was headed straight back out for another corner. I changed my position to the front post, which was in touching distance of the fans behind the goal, when one of them shouted: 'Whatever, Carlisle. You'll always be a fucking Dingle.'

Looking round I saw dozens of chuckling faces and, with a big cheesy grin on my own, I replied: 'Yeah, a rich Dingle.'

Jeers and laughs enveloped the group and we got on with the game. I love things like this. I know it's easy to go straight to the money aspect of football, and to play up to the reputation that footballers have, but I think if you say it with a smile on your face and don't swan around like you are Charlie Charles Charles you can get away with it.

Another easy line to put down the hecklers is to infer a sexual conquest very close to home. I have to admit that these responses are slightly more risky, because you don't know what their personal circumstances are and the last thing you want is to strike an insensitive chord if there's been some sort of tragedy. But I think most people, especially in this environment, accept it for what it is and the spirit it's intended. I utilised this approach at Sixfields one day. We were defending a corner this time, in front of the away fans, when a deep voice shouted out: 'Carlisle, you're fucking shit.'

'That's not what your mum said,' I replied. The whoops and jeers put smiles all round and we all got on with the game. Another twist on the 'cash shot' came later in the season and I wrote a blog about it, which read like this:

A Boot Room With A View . . .

Good evening all and welcome to my new blog!

I've often been told that 'good news is no news' and, to be honest, I'm sick of it. Why does everything have to be sensationalist, scandalous or just downright smutty? Well, I'm here to buck that trend. I'll hopefully tell you about good things that are happening in the game and give some balance to very lopsided perception.

Soccer star embroiled in 'enjoyable banter' shock!

At a time when questions are being asked about the line between 'banter' and 'abuse', let me tell you about Monday night. I'm playing in the FA Cup first round replay for York City away at AFC Wimbledon, and it's live on ESPN. We get a corner in front of the home fans and, as usual, the big ugly lumps come striding forward to add our unrefined yet significant aerial prowess to the attack. As I line up at the front post the whole stand breaks into song:

'He plays like he's pissed
He plays like he's pi-issed
That Clarke Carlisle
He plays like he's pissed'

It was all I could do to stop laughing there and then. I've made no secret of my past, of the mistakes I've made and what I've done to correct them, so I knew I would get something like this from time to time; it just had to happen when it was live on the bloody telly! Not long later, there was a break in play while someone got treatment for an injury and I walked over to the dugout to get a drink. As I quenched my thirst a lone voice shot out of the crowd:

'Oi, Carlisle, where's your motor?'

A very well angled dig at the fact that I'd lost my licence. So good, in fact, that I actually bit back at this one . . .

'Which one?' I shouted back. 'The Porsche or the Merc?!'

A little jeer went up around him and smiles were on everybody's face. Before you lambast me for my arrogance, I don't even have a car, but that wasn't the point. It was great to get involved in an amicable way, to show that I am human, I can hear you and I do appreciate the funny side.

This is where I think social media comes into full effect. Many players are on sites like Twitter, Facebook and such like, and many use them to great effect. The days are long gone where players travel on the bus to matches with fans (although I have been alongside a few on the trains this last year), or have a pint in the local with them afterwards (although I did try and resurrect this tradition once or twice), but the technological distance between us all is just one button click. That gap between player and fan has been bridged and it is fantastic for us all. As long as every-one remembers that there are human beings on the other side of those screens: players, fans, adults, kids, men, women, boys and girls. Your screen might be faceless, but your reader is not . . .

I am sure that some fans think that being part of a crowd gives them complete anonymity, and absolves them of any culpability for what they say. They know that it is highly unlikely for the stewards or police to bring them to task about what they say, and the players will never get involved, especially after what happened with Eric Cantona back in 1995. Well, many have found that I am not 'normal' when it comes to the classification of people, and definitely abnormal when it comes to reactions in certain situations.

One incident provided me and my team-mates with a good chuckle, but actually resulted in a far more interesting outcome much further down the line. It was a match at Deepdale and we were trudging off the pitch after a very underwhelming draw against opposition that we 'should' have been beating. The tunnel is in the corner of the ground and the home fans from two stands can congregate around it to make you either strut through a guard of honour or cower through a walk of shame. After that day's result we were bracing ourselves to run the gauntlet.

I had been a sub for the game, so reached the tunnel in close proximity to the manager, Phil Brown, who was bearing the brunt of the disaffection. Even when you haven't been on the pitch, you can still often be the subject of arbitrary tirades of abuse, and today was no different. After finishing his volley at the gaffer, one fan saw me coming and leant over the advertising hoardings to launch a frothymouthed verbal assault on me. Like I said, I'm not 'most players', and I decided that this was a tad uncalled-for, so I turned back, walked straight over to the guy in question and simply asked: 'I beg your pardon, what was that?'

The raging bull terrier instantly turned into a trembling poodle: 'I'm, er, no, er, I mean, what I was trying to say was, erm, it just wasn't good enough.'

'I appreciate that, but was that my fault? I didn't even play.'

'Er, yes, I mean, no, well, you've not been outstanding all

the time and I know you've played in the Premier League and I, well, I just want us to win.'

'And do you think I, or we, don't want to win?'

'Well, er, no, but sometimes it just doesn't look like it.'

'I appreciate that, but does that mean you launch abuse at me and us like dogs?'

'Well, no, sorry about that, I'm just angry.'

'No worries, I understand. Just know that we want to win, too.'

And with that I trotted down the tunnel. There was further conversation on Twitter where his friends named him and took the mickey about the whole situation. I was very proud about how I dealt with it. I confronted him in a non-aggressive way and actually personalised his behaviour. I am not a robot that moronically ploughs its way through life but, like I keep reiterating, a fellow human being. When that gets brought to people's attention it seems that attitudes do change quite dramatically. After the game, we had a chuckle about it in the dressing room, and I thought nothing more about it until some 14 to 16 months down the line when I received an email that completely surprised me.

In it, my abuser wrote to apologise for his behaviour that day, hoping that his comments hadn't caused me any distress – especially as he had subsequently heard about my battles with depression. He'd been so concerned that he'd tried to meet me at Beacon Fell, where the team often trained, so that he could apologise in person, and he'd sent me some positive tweets applauding my performances. He said that he had even had sleepless nights worrying about it all. He concluded by saying: 'While I do not expect you to forgive my actions, I do hope you realise the extent to which I am truly sorry for my behaviour . . . Clarke Carlisle is not just a footballer, but a fellow human being. You deserved to be treated with far more respect than I showed you on that day and I am truly sorry for that.'

Wow, this blew me away. To think that a situation I had left long in the past had affected someone else so greatly was a real eye-opener. I wonder if other fans would hold a mirror to their actions and behaviours if they were made to see the human impact? What I thought was slightly more troubling was the fact that many players don't go through the very cathartic process that I did in this situation. They probably trudge past their abusers, head down, and digest what is said in their own way and in their own time. I wonder how many players have been affected by these taunts, which are in truth little more than an overt display of frustration and anger by supporters at the lack of success of the team they follow, and rarely intended as an actual direct attack on the individual concerned? Far more than readily admit it, I'm sure. I did reassure this guy that there weren't any residual effects on me from our *tête à tête*, and I hope he feels better for knowing that, but what the whole episode does show is that you just never know how deep and far-reaching the repercussions of your actions can be.

However, don't assume that it is only fans who can hold illogical perceptions of players and teams. Professional footballers can do, too – after all, we are a competitive bunch, and you don't get far in the game without having a fair degree of confidence in your own abilities. I was in the car with three of my team-mates and we were talking about the weekend's Premier League results. Aston Villa had been fielding a very young side and their results weren't comfortable reading for any Villa fan. One of my team-mates thought he'd identified one reason for their struggles: 'Bannan's shit,' he said, referring to Villa's young midfielder who already had more than 50 Premier League games under his belt, not to mention a dozen or so caps for Scotland.

Comments like this always make me laugh. He can't be that shit, he's getting picked every week in the Prem. And who is that judgement in comparison to? You or Ronaldo? To be fair to my team-mate, he is not alone in making comments like this.

Chris Eagles held damning views on the majority of players in the top flight. After spending many a session arguing with him over the validity of his point, I think I realised where it comes from. Most of those he condemned were players that he either played with or against a lot as a young player. Chris's point of reference was five years earlier, when he was being tipped by some to become the next Ryan Giggs and he was waltzing rings around a lot of these guys for United. The difference now is that they have progressed, but he still sees them as the chumps he used to take the mickey out of. Professional envy, it can be an ugly thing.

CHAPTER 9 —

THE VIEW FROM THE BENCH

At the beginning of November, we played AFC Wimbledon three times in nine days, with a league fixture sandwiched in between an FA Cup tie and a replay. The league game ended in a resounding 3-0 defeat and in the dressing room at the final whistle the manager launched a full-scale inquiry. I was surprised at how worked up he was, as this was our first defeat after six games unbeaten, but nevertheless he wanted to call a crisis meeting. 'Don't panic, Mr Mainwaring!' was all I could think, but I obviously didn't say it out loud.

It's funny how the cracks in your performances get papered over and ignored when you're winning games, or at least not losing. It often happens in football that teams win games without playing particularly well. How many times do you hear pundits talk of 'grinding out results'? When this is happening, it is very easy for certain actions or performances to be overlooked. Mistakes that have led to goals being conceded can be looked at humorously, because the team managed to rescue the situation by scoring more at the other end. It's when the results don't materialise that you see the true measure of a squad and its staff. The gaffer opened the floor for comments and some very interesting points came forward. The lads raised the issue of negative shouting and said that the anxiety coming from the bench whenever the players did anything wrong was proving detrimental to their play.

'Oh, so it's *my* fault, is it?!' exclaimed the boss angrily. A laughable back and forth ensued between players and staff, with some lads making points, then immediately back-tracking or stumbling over an explanation. It was as if they had summoned the courage to say something and then immediately regretted the decision to do so. Coaches Des Lyttle and Darron Gee (known as GeeBo) were standing in the doorway to the showers, harrumphing and chuntering under their breath all the while, shaking their heads in disgust whenever they were mentioned in any of the players' observations.

You might think that this sort of clear-the-air debate would help, but I have only ever been in two dressing rooms where there has been any use whatsoever in voicing honest opinions – they were with Aidy Boothroyd at Watford and Phil Brown at Preston. These guys listened to your opinions (whether they acted on them or not was another matter), but at least they didn't do what every other manager I've played under has done, and used your words as ammunition the next time something goes wrong.

For example, I remember how we mentioned to one manager that his training was far too intense the day before a game. He changed the schedule the following week and we lost 1-0, at which he launched into a diatribe about us all being lazy, selfish good-for-nothings. The following week he worked us harder than ever the day before the game; we lost

4-0. Another manager asked one of the lads for his opinion about a player he was thinking of taking on loan. The player duly arrived and, when given his debut, had an absolute stinker. After the game the manager gave the loanee a real verbal volley, which he concluded with: 'And he doesn't like you [pointing at the guy he'd asked for a reference]. He thinks you're a pussy, he told me before you came. I don't agree, I think you're a c**t.'

What the hell kind of a place is it to work in where that is your level of appraisal? I wish there was a fly on the wall of all dressing rooms – there would be some serious bans flying around. In this discussion at York, though, the lads do have a point. If you are going to tell your team to play expansive passing football, you can't then lambast them when they make an error passing the ball, or scream from the sidelines during the game to 'Get rid of it'. Doing so just contradicts everything you are telling them during the week. It confuses the team even more when one coach is shouting for one thing to be done and the other is shouting for you to do something completely different. Mixed messages from the bench breed uncertainty in the team, and that is in danger of happening here.

Some coaches have a habit of seeing what they want to see, too. Michael Potts was on the receiving end of a classic example of this. I watched a training session where he did seven or eight good things in a row, made correct decisions and executed them well. He then gave away one pass and the session was instantly halted.

'Pottsy, Pottsy, Pottsy. What the fuck are you doing, man? Just give it simple. That's why you don't fucking play – just do it simple.'

I shook my head when I heard that. I'm all for coaching and highlighting errors, but it needs to be done with a bit of balance. If the coaches just remembered to compliment him as the session carried on, it would be a start. Once someone categorises you, it is very hard to break away from that and change people's perceptions. This is why some players need a 'fresh start' every now and again, and I think Pottsy might be in that group.

Players can react so differently when they are out of the team. The want and need to play on a Saturday is inherent in you, so when that goes unfulfilled it can lead to emotional responses of varying degrees. Some players completely toss it off, time-keeping, training, the lot. They take their omission from the starting line-up as a direct and personal slight against their character. I was with one player who used to exact his revenge in training, intentionally topping anyone who came within a five-yard radius.

Some guys become extremely moody and low. I can understand this, because it is so difficult to stop your mind from projecting into the future. You start wondering if you'll ever get back in the side, if the manager has finally decided that you're not for him. You ask yourself questions such as: what if I don't get offered another contract now? What will I do? Where will I go? The ramifications of being out of the side can have seriously adverse effects on your future. Your earning capacity goes down, people ask questions about why you're not in the side, and you fear the answers they come up with will put you in a bad light.

Others have an appreciation for the nature of what is now a squad industry. There will be times when you are out of the team for one reason or another – injury, loss of form, suspension – and you just have to keep your head down and work hard until your next chance arrives. I usually fall into this category. There are times when I really want to throw one in, but I try to ignore those voices in my head. Wherever I go, they are always there with me. But instead I continue to train to the best of my ability, often actually doing a little more, tackling a little harder and running a little further than necessary, just to try to put myself back on the manager's radar.

I find it much harder to deal with a match day, though, especially when I'm a sub. There is a high chance that you will be involved if you are a forward player, even a midfielder, but defenders and goalkeepers have two hopes of getting on, unless there is an injury in the game. To add a little more weight to it all, you are in a lose-lose situation because all you can do is mess up. Coming on with ten minutes to go is horrible: make a mistake and you let everyone down; help the team hold out and your contribution is barely recognised. I am desperate to be a moody sub, be Bad Santa and throw the toys out of my pram, but I just can't. I still end up encouraging the others and working hard; it's really quite annoying.

It can also spark an emotional reaction to be subbed off. I've seen water bottles kicked, boots thrown and handshakes ignored, but the most notable response was from one lad who was subbed off at half time. He got showered, dressed and walked out of the ground to the pub next door. He ordered a pint and sat down to watch the second half in there, absolutely bothered. I am not professing to be a saint by any stretch of the imagination. At the height of my frustrations at Burnley when I was out of the side, I used to duck out of the back of the stand and have a smoke with the stewards. Like I said, I've made many bad choices.

The bench at York is just like every other I've ever sat on, made up of a mixture of these characters. The final dimension to the atmosphere created here is the behaviour of the staff. The animation of the manager and coaches, or lack of it, can have a significant impact on what is happening in front of them. I have been fortunate enough to spend the majority of my career actually on the pitch, and from there you can generally blank out the inane ramblings that come from the dugout. There are occasions, however, especially when the bench is on your side of the pitch, when you just can't get away from them.

Managers such as Ian Holloway and Aidy Boothroyd will ensure that you hear them. If you don't (or if you pretend not to) you will get both barrels in the dressing room, so it is often easier just to acknowledge their calls at the time. Some managers seem to keep on saying the same things, no matter what is happening. For example, Owen Coyle's stock phrase was 'track your runners', which was pretty much the only thing I ever heard him say when I was on the pitch. At the other end of the scale is a manager such as Brian Laws, who didn't say a dickie bird for the duration of the game.

There is a marked difference between coaching from the sideline and shouting arbitrary comments from there. When the game is mid-flow, it is probably the worst time to try to chastise your players. Players don't mean to make mistakes. No player goes out with the intention of missing the target, misplacing a pass or losing the ball; they are mistakes and the player knows it. If you choose to berate him at the top of your voice in front of all the players, fans and watching millions, it is likely to cause him anxiety and shame, and will induce selective hearing to anything else you have to say.

Sitting on the bench for York for one or two games made the impact of negativity from the bench completely apparent to me. GeeBo and Des Lyttle are two very vocal characters. They are the chorus leaders when a mistake is made, either by calling the player out, cussing at the top of their voices or just giving an exaggerated 'humph' for the world to see. As much as I try to keep quiet, I just can't. I would dearly love to take them to task on the spot, in front of the crowd in exactly the same way that they are dressing down the team, but that would be plain disrespectful. Instead, I give louder shouts of positivity and encouragement.

'Well done, Chambo!'

'Hard lines, Jase. Next one's in the top bin.'

'Keep them going, Smudger. It's going to come.'

The acknowledgement of these shouts comes far more readily and it looks to me as though their reaction is one of head up, chest out, which I think is much better for us as a team and for them as individuals. Don't get me wrong, we will address the errors that have been made and how to improve the team, but the place for this is in the dressing room at half time or after the game when it can be done in a constructive way. The more I listened, the more it became apparent that the coaches weren't even shouting the same things. One of them was trying to get the lads to pass the ball while the other wanted them to play long, in the channels.

There aren't many more confusing things than getting mixed messages from your own staff. You can never do right for doing wrong. To have an identity as a team, you have to endorse the same message from all of the staff, and continually reinforce it whether it is working or not. You can't encourage players to pass the ball, but then lambast them if the passing breaks down and they concede. You have to applaud the fact that they were trying to do the right thing and encourage them to go again.

This is why Swansea have been so successful. You will see their passing game get them into trouble on about half a dozen occasions a season, but you don't see any drastic reactions from their manager or any change in their style; they press forward with their ideals and thus have created an identity, one that has made the Liberty Stadium quite a feared place to travel to.

I can see the effect that all of these slightly mixed messages is having on some of our players. Ashley Chambers, Matty Blair, Michael Coulson and Jason Walker are our key attacking options. They are players with excellent technical ability and they will wreak havoc in this league, as long as they are free to do so. We are not even into November and they have already begun to ignore what is being said from the bench and have very unconfident body language. It is something we'll have to keep an eye on.

CHAPTER 10

STIFFS AND STINKERS

I have never been fond of reserve matches. They're a tangible indication that you are not good enough, something that no player ever wants to consider. The only time they are tolerable is when you are playing to regain your match fitness. After being out for three weeks, I would normally feel that I was in desperate need of a run-out before getting back into the first team. With the way my body responded to a summer off and then being thrown in at the deep end, I'm not altogether convinced it's necessary this time, but it is still part of the standard club routine. It is a chance to get your fitness levels back, test your injury out in something akin to a competitive scenario, and also show the manager that you are of a good, professional character.

This last trait is quite often the more important to a manager when these games come around. The modern-day footballer is his own biggest fan. I have never known a player who doesn't think that he should be in the first XI – even some of the apprentices have this delusion. So when a reserve fixture comes along, there is often a tendency to put in sub-maximal effort, or even make excuses not to play. However, if a manager sees that a player is unhappy turning out at Dog and Duck Park to play in front of one man and his dog, but still applies himself like it's a first team game, it leaves a lasting impression. As far as I can remember, I have always been disappointed about playing for the reserves. I have always grumbled to myself about why I'm there, maybe even discussed it with a few of the lads, but when it actually comes to the game I am confronted by that bloody voice in my head again.

'Are you just going to toss this off?'

'Who do you think you are?'

'What if this is your last ever game, away at Chorley, pissing down, freezing, and you just tossed it off?'

'These kids will probably run you ragged even if you did try.'

Bollocks. Right, someone's going to get it. I am going to smash someone, head everything, and if the gaffer's watching he'll have to put me back in the side. Let's go!

It wasn't that straightforward to get to this conclusion today, when Gary Mills had arranged a game for the reserves against Newcastle's academy lads. There was a gale blowing across the training ground, it was pissing down with rain, freezing cold and altogether not a very nice place to play against the Toon's next generation of superstars. I really wanted to wear some gloves, but the gaffer was in attendance and I thought it might go against the tough centre-half image I was hoping to convey. It was actually really refreshing that all of our lads came to the same conclusion on this occasion, and these pups from the Northeast were a tad perturbed by our commitment and intensity.

'Watch out, it's only a friendly!' exclaimed their striker when I scythed him down.

Offering a hand to pick him up, I casually educated him about the world of football. 'There's no such thing as a friendly, son.'

I don't know if he expected me to just stand back and let him try all his tricks and flicks and then allow him to run around with the freedom of York. No way, José, I am going to get stuck into him and make this as easy an afternoon as possible for me. All over the park this was going on, to the point where these young men were so het up they came out with two classic, petulant shouts: 'I probably earn more than you' and, the even more misguided, 'You play for York because you're shit'.

Oh, my dear boy, I've played more league games this season than you are likely to in your entire career, and I'll remind you of that when you're serving me in Nando's in three years' time. The effect of his taunt was also somewhat reduced with the word 'probably' in there. If you're going to cash someone off, at least be confident about it.

I'm not going to pretend that there weren't big-time Charlies when I was an apprentice or young pro; of course there were, but even the biggest of Billy Big Bollocks held a modicum of respect for senior pros. It doesn't seem to be par for the course any more, and this was highlighted after the game by one of the most disheartening things I've seen for a long time in this regard.

Their team had made the journey down on one of those five-star corporate hospitality luxury coaches, and they had all plonked themselves back on it, listening to their iPods and gadgets. Behind them, pushing the kit skips to the bus all by himself, was Peter Beardsley. Yes, *the* Peter Beardsley. I couldn't catch my breath. When I was a YT, it was all part of our apprenticeship to do the kit, boots, push skips and make coffees; the generations before me would probably have bloody carried Peter Beardsley to the bus, but that level of respect is just not there any more. Peter actually apologised to our management team for the behaviour of some of his players, that's how disconcerting it was to him. How times change.

I'm just over a month into my time with York and things have been, well, interesting. I haven't exactly set the world alight, but then again I feel I've performed admirably well considering I had done no previous training, save for the couple of runs during and after Greece. The injury had really curtailed any momentum that I felt I was gaining and being on the bench for the last three games has instigated the self-deprecating appraisal that my mind is so familiar with: 'This was a very bad decision. You should have made retirement work. You'll never get back in the team now. Is this going to be how you go out? As a washed-up journeyman who can't get into York's team.'

What a tonic it was, then, to see a former manager's name light up my phone on a gloomy October Monday morning. I sincerely hope that this is the call I think it is, the 'general catch-up, just seeing how you're getting on' conversation, that really means: 'Are you happy? Do you want to sign for us?' I'm glad that it's this manager in particular, as he doesn't mess about.

In such a guarded industry, it's refreshing to be able to speak openly and honestly to a manager, especially a prospective manager, about how you're feeling, what your situation is and what you want to do. With most managers, these discussions are usually full of the same old bullshit: 'Oh, it's great here, I'm great, you're great.' But with Aidy Boothroyd I don't have to go there. I told him that he was correct, which he was, that things weren't feeling exactly right at the time. When I advised him of my plans to try to retire in the summer, he immediately rang the alarm. Everybody associated with football tells you to think twice before quitting the game as you are a long time retired. It seems to be a stock phrase almost on a par with 'a game of two halves', but Aidy has a greater insight than that.

'Have you read the book *Rich Dad, Poor Dad*?' he asked me, which I hadn't. He believed it would give me a sense of clarity in my situation. I must confess that I still haven't read it to date, so I can't say if it would help or not, but he has always been right in his other observations and suggestions. In the past, he has made recommendations such as Sun Tzu's *The Art of War* and various other books that address the topics of mindset, psyche and application. They have all contributed to how I have moulded my approach to life.

With this in mind, I should have placed greater credence on his approach months before, but I was quite belligerent in my thoughts. At the time, his guidance just further cemented my decision to go the other way. Yet again, my determination to go against the grain and prove people wrong had forged my destiny. Before this season, however, I had to admit defeat. When I had finally reached this conclusion, it had been too late to salvage the contract offer I'd had from Northampton ahead of the start of the campaign. I have to confess that it pained me somewhat to admit that, not least because it had cost me financially, too. I told Aidy as much, but I also told him of the positives. At York, football had become enjoyable again. You cannot replace the euphoric feelings of a match, the emotional rollercoaster of the 90-minute experience which is the culmination of a week's preparation and drive. It was good to be involved.

He asked whether I had discussed with York what was to happen beyond January, which we hadn't, so he requested to be kept in the loop. I would happily do this for two reasons. Firstly, I need elaborate no further on the respect that I have for Aidy, and this would just be an extension of that. Secondly, it is always good to have two (or more) interested parties when it comes to contract negotiations. The ability to play one off against the other is a huge advantage when it comes to getting the best deal. This is the self-preservation society.

A week or so later, Aidy called again, so I think it's safe to say that there might be a bit more in this than just general interest. I know that he signed Dave Artell in the summer when I passed up on his offer. I don't want to sound arrogant, but I don't think he would have brought him in if I'd signed. That's nothing to do with talent, as Dave is a steady centre-half like myself, yet he has much more ability with the ball at his feet, which was why he fitted into the Crewe Alexandra set-up so well. He obviously gets stuck in, too; either that or he had a very tough paper round in the cobbled Yorkshire streets.

My reasoning is that I'm sure Aidy wouldn't play two aging centre-halves in the same team (Dave is only a year younger than me). He wouldn't play me and Malky Mackay together for the simple reason that we were too easily undone by pace. There has to be someone in his defensive pairing that has the ability to put out fires with their pace. That is why it was always Malky or myself alongside Danny Shittu or Jay Demerit. There was 'disaster prevention' in one player, 'disaster recovery' in the other. And at the time, I wouldn't have imagined that Northampton would have the budget to afford Aidy the luxury of signing both of us, especially when one or the other wouldn't play. Now that Northampton are below us in the league, which Aidy won't be happy about, perhaps he has the opportunity to bring in someone else to bolster their side. So maybe I have landed on my feet after all? Everything happens for a reason, or is it that there is a reason for everything happening?

As I was saying earlier, when you come on as a substitute defender, you are in a lose-lose situation and last night I lost-lost! It was the Johnstone's Paint Trophy and we were playing against Coventry City at home. Coventry are in the league above us, but the boys had battered them in the first half and should have been at least two goals up at the break. The underdogs were buoyant coming out for the second half and the bench was in good spirits. A couple of minutes in and one of the centre-halves, Chris Doig, pulled up with a muscle injury. I was coming on.

I am usually very composed in these situations. I know that I need to get up to speed with the game, so I try to make sure that I do my basics well for the first five minutes, by which I mean simply heading and kicking the ball. I don't try anything too fancy, no wonder passes or quick feet in my own box, just keep it simple and get into the game. It could well have been my first touch of the ball. Our keeper, Michael Ingham, rolled the ball out to me in the right-back position, where I took a touch and tried to pass it inside to my fellow centre-half, Smudger. I looked up to see David

McGoldrick leisurely stroll on to my pass and slot the ball in the far corner – 1-0. I could quite happily have walked straight back off the pitch; it was a disgusting start. I knew I was going to need some help, and quickly, to get through this.

'Okay, you've had an absolute shitter, but that's all right, just make sure you get your next job right. You've got forty minutes to totally redeem yourself, just get the next one right.'

Buggerfuck, it was just one of those days. The more I tried, the worse I got. I was mistiming headers, running into my own team-mates, and couldn't pass water never mind the ball. The game ended up 4-0 and I was in some way at fault for every goal. It was the mother of all Reggie Blinkers, so bad in fact that I couldn't even go back through it in my own head afterwards. I just had to bury that one deep, maybe even into Pandora's Box, for me to assess in counselling one day.

I say that, but as I make my way to work the next day I know that everyone knows that I was terrible. We lost that game and it was entirely my fault. The only way to deal with it is to 'fake it to make it'. I've just got to bowl in like it doesn't matter a jot, big smile on my face and the same enthusiasm that I greet every other day with. I did my usual round of handshakes, high-fives and hearty good mornings, and maintained a general buzz around the place. One of the younger lads, Pottsy, asked me how I can do it.

'Do what?' I asked

'Be so happy after that game?'

'I've had more Reggie Blinkers than you've had hot dinners, Pottsy lad. That wasn't the first and it will definitely not be the last. It doesn't make me a bad player! Today is a new day, I'm alive and I'm a professional footballer, what is there to not be happy about?'

'I love you Clarkey, that's brilliant!'

And that is exactly how it should be. The reality is that I am hurting because of my performance, but no one's died, I am still here and I have a chance to put it right in how I train and how I play the next game, if selected, which is by no means certain after that. It is also true that it's not the first time I've had a bad game. There have been so many others where I just could not do the right thing. One that sticks out in my mind was for Burnley in the Premier League. There was an added twist to this one because I was already the centre of attention for entirely non-footballing reasons.

Earlier in the season I had fulfilled one of my lifelong ambitions, to appear on *Countdown*. I love the show. I had been watching it since I was a wee nipper, on my dad's knee, having a kiddie crush on Carol Vorderman and not under-standing the late, great Richard Whiteley's banter. I had applied to go on the show back in 2002, when I was out with my knee injury, but I failed the audition at a dingy hotel near Euston station. That didn't sway me from my belief that I could win on the show. The audition was just a group of people seated around a table who had letters read out to them by someone at the top of the table. It was noth-ing like the show.

I thrive on the format, on the pressure of the clock tick-ing, and am used to working with the layout of the big blue and white cards on the TV. I have never played with a pad and paper before. That's not strictly true. There was a period when I made it a three-player game, with me playing against the two on the TV. I kept score on a pad as though it were real. I'm telling you, I loved the show. I generally won four out of five shows, and kept telling Mrs C as much. I'm surprised she is still with me.

My opportunity to appear on the programme came about by pure chance. I had mentioned in an interview on talk-SPORT radio that I had always wanted to appear on the show. Unbeknown to me, one of the producers at the station was also a producer on *Countdown*. He rang me and asked if I was serious.

'Does Rambo carry a knife?'

I was deadly serious. And so it came to pass. I absolutely loved it. I have never been as nervous in all my life as when we were recording the first episode. All of the fear of embarrassment, failure and the ramifications of these were putting me in a full body sweat. My mouth was dry but my top lip was not. Thrive on the format? I positively shat myself! I won a show and that was all that mattered. I actually went on to win a second in a much more relaxed and confident manner, and when I was 21 points up in the third I thought I was destined to become an octo-champ.

The biggest regret of my TV life is losing that third show. The conundrum, 'STEAMIEST', will forever stain my memory, but that doesn't actually haunt me. The pivotal score was in the very first round. To my surprise my opponent declared a five-letter word. I had several sixes, a seven and a risky eight. Instead of opting for the safe point-scorer, 'CASINO' or even 'CARRION', I plumped for 'CARRIONS', pluralising a mass noun. Rather than be 7-0 up from the off, I was 5-0 down, a 12-point swing that would have rendered the final conundrum irrelevant. I still dream about it, and it still hurts.

The programmes were aired a couple of months later and there was an element of hysteria in the amount of press attention I received from it. This was doing wonders for my profile until that following Saturday when we had a Premier League relegation six-pointer against Portsmouth at home. I didn't just fall from a great height, I plummeted. I was at fault for two goals and gave away a penalty, which fortunately was saved, but we lost the game nevertheless. My antics of the previous week were the perfect fuel for all and sundry to completely dismantle me.

'I've got a nine letter word for you: "RELEGATED".'

Even the guys on *Match of the Day* got in on the act: 'How about: "NIGHTMARE"?'

The only thing that annoyed me was that a number of fans thought I had been missing training that week to go and record the shows. Utterly oblivious to the fact that they were recorded months earlier, they let me have both barrels, and I just had to take it. My performance was so bad there was no point in trying to defend myself; I had to take this one on the chin and go and put it right next time I went out there. I'm sure fans of the various clubs I've been at will readily recall plenty of other bad games that I've played, but this is definitely the one that stands front and centre for me.

Back at training after the York v Coventry game the manager, Gary Mills, left a message for me to call him. He wanted to talk to me about my preparation, check that I was doing everything okay and to mark my card.

'A performance like that is not good enough for my team, Clarke.'

I really admired how forthright he was and the fact that

he had the balls to tell me straight up. I explained that there was no reason for it other than a bad day at the office. He went on to question my behaviour on the bench and with the opposition before/during matches.

'You're always smiling and joking on the bench. Is that professional? And why do you keep shaking hands with the enemy, giving players hugs and stuff? Is that right Clarke? You know, I don't think that's right.'

This is one part of the industry that I have had to change my mentality about. The opposition aren't 'the enemy', they're fellow professionals, fellow members who are doing their job just like me. I have adapted my approach so that I now feel I can greet and interact with guys as fellow human beings. That doesn't mean I won't head their heads when there's a ball to be won. Ask any striker in League 2 that I've played against this year. We have enjoyed the game in a professional and respectful way, but they all know they were in a battle. If it moves, I kick it. If it doesn't move, I kick it until it does. Win, lose or draw, we are playing the greatest game in the world and getting paid for it. I am getting so close to the end of my career, I am not going to waste any of it. I will play every game as though it is my last, with a smile on my face and a fire in my belly. There isn't a manager in the world who can take that out of me.

CHAPTER 11

PART OF THE UNION

There's a storm brewing in the football world. It is the Kick It Out 'weeks of action' campaign and a few players are threatening to boycott it. Kick It Out is an anti-discrimination initiative that works in the world of football. It initially began as Kick Racism Out Of Football, but as it broadened its horizons to cover more areas of discrimination, the name was changed. In the weeks of action, different activities take place up and down the country which are intended to challenge discrimination in all its forms and promote inclusion in all facets of the game. The 'money shot' in the context of promotion is a weekend of fixtures where every professional player up and down the country wears a Kick It Out t-shirt to symbolise football's total support for the cause.

The scheduled date for this is imminent and there are rumours circulating that a few players may not join in this show of support because they don't feel that the campaign is working effectively. I have to say that at this point I am not entirely sure what it will achieve to not wear the t-shirt. KIO have been at the forefront of change over the past

30 years, and in that time we have seen dramatic changes in the battle against racism. They are one of a few bodies who are actually doing something positive about the issue. I would suggest that if there is a point to be made, then make it to those who can truly effect change, such as FIFA, UEFA and the FA here in England, not a small charitable initiative that works with a budget of under £500,000 and has approximately ten staff.

A couple of the lads at York said that they wouldn't be wearing their t-shirts so, in a completely neutral manner, I asked them why. They said that they were sick of incidents being swept under the carpet, that the authorities don't take the issue seriously and that the punishments handed out to John Terry for his comments to Anton Ferdinand and to Luis Suarez for what he said to Patrice Evra were laughable. I told them that I completely respected their opinions, and that they have views that are shared by many, but asked whether this was all the fault of KIO? A resounding no came forth from all. I explained my view and said that I would voice my concerns (in my role as chairman of the PFA) over how the issue is dealt with and the problems with the process, but I would do it to those who are responsible for the absolute calamities that have gone before – such as the fact that some governing bodies have been fined just a few thousand euros for incidents of serious racial abuse. It will be interesting to see if they do wear the t-shirt or not, and how many others join in.

Little did I realise that things were about to blow up again, and this suddenly became a very intense week. What was initially going to be a couple of leisurely TV appearances morphed into something quite different. It began with a bit of studio work for ESPN. The England Under-21s were playing their final match in the qualification campaign for the European Championships. It was away in Serbia and I was in the studio in Chiswick with Paul Ince to do the punditry for the game. Paul's son, Thomas, was playing in the match. England scored in the final seconds of the match to seal qualification and, as can be expected at such a joyous time, celebrated with great gusto. Suddenly, all hell broke loose. There was a huge brawl in the middle of the pitch involving players and staff from both sides. Kicks, punches and head-butts were being thrown, players were being wrestled – it was total chaos. I was astonished at what I was seeing.

'Get out of there, son. GET OUT OF THERE!' screamed Paul at the monitor.

Oh my days! I can't imagine how he is feeling having to watch this from here. What a desperately sad situation to find yourself in. He must feel so helpless, seeing his son in the middle of it yet powerless to do anything about it. This is truly awful.

It transpired that the players had been racially abused by the crowd during the match, something that wasn't entirely clear on the broadcast transmission. Because some of the England players were so upset by what they were hearing during the game, they celebrated with greater fervour than they might have done otherwise, and this caused the players to confront each other and violence ensued. This is 2013. What on earth is going on? How can this still be happening on such a scale and so overtly in this day and age? More to the point, what are UEFA going to do about it? I can bet my bottom dollar that they don't do anything as severe as the

100,000 euro fine and one-match ban they gave to Nicklas Bendtner for his breach of advertising rules when he revealed the name of a bookmaker on his underpants after scoring a goal in Euro 2012. There is a disgusting disparity between the sanctions imposed for offences that will cost the governing body money and those that are unethical or immoral. FIFA and UEFA appear to value the cash far higher than they value the integrity and image of the game – their fine system tells us so.

I had a day of interviews scheduled for later in the week at Media City which were supposed to be about the upcoming KIO weeks of action, but they have been gazumped by this event and the threatened boycott. It's a tough balancing act to support your members' actions when you disagree with them. I agree with the fact that racism is still an issue that needs a complete change in the way it is tackled, but I disagree that to make this point we should boycott a campaign that is working so hard in this area. We have to call on the power-mongers to get their hands dirty, stop pussyfooting around the issue and get some direct and visible action started. I hope I have managed to strike the balance.

In the event, there were quite a few players who didn't wear the KIO t-shirts this weekend, though my two team-mates did. The whole Swansea and Wigan teams didn't wear them (reportedly to show solidarity with those who didn't want to wear them), and nor did Anton and Rio Ferdinand, along with Joleon Lescott and Jason Roberts. Actually, Lescott hasn't worn his t-shirt for many years now, allegedly due to the way an incident was handled some time ago.

The result of this is that my phone is ringing off the hook

with calls from any and every possible media outlet. I would have thought that the BBC would need only one interview, but no, they need one for BBC News, *BBC Breakfast*, Radios 1, 2, 3, 4 and 5, Lancashire, Merseyside, Three Counties and every other bloody station in between. Have they not learnt how to cut and paste?!

I am so disappointed that all players couldn't have joined together to wear the shirts; it seems as though I have failed to get people to unite and support the cause. Furthermore, I feel under attack from a group of players who are questioning my position, my representation of them and the issue. This has really hurt me. Why on God's earth have they thrown this at me now? Where the hell have they been for the past eight years, when I've seen the same faces at the anti-racism initiatives? I could count on my fingers the guys who've been to the KIO and Show Racism the Red Card workshops and meetings. From my viewpoint, it seems as though they can't be arsed to join in, because it's inconvenient to attend on a day off, or too much for them to contribute after training, but they readily gun me down for giving my opinion on the subject.

I wouldn't mind if people disagreed, or they had other points of view they wanted to make, but I had given everyone the perfect, global platform to do so when I made my documentary *Is Football Racist?*. Where were they then? I let people know that I was making the documentary, but no one wanted to join in. We desperately tried to get players to take part in the programme and tell us about their frustrations, about what they have experienced and what they would like to see done about it, but no one had the balls to take part other than Jermaine Jenas and my boys at Northampton.

Rather than speaking out and addressing the topic full on to explain why they are upset or concerned, a few people decided to do something as trivial as to not wear a t-shirt, before melting back into the crowd. What does that actually say? How can football fans understand the point they are making when they are not giving their reasons properly.

It pisses me right off. I've had to stand up and try to represent everyone in a balanced way, being damned if I do and damned if I don't. It's not them and their wives getting abuse on Twitter from all sides of the issue. I can pretty much guarantee that no one other than Jason Roberts will say something publicly. However, the Premier League 'big' players will happily throw in a grenade by not wearing a t-shirt, but when it explodes they won't do anything, appearing to hide behind their 'advisers'. That's because they're shithouses. Now that they have made their 'statement' for all to see, how many will stand up in front of the cameras and be counted?

This whole situation is getting crazier by the day. There are now rumblings of a Black Players' Union being established. I could not think of a worse possible idea. In this fight against racism, how can you create something that instantly divides the membership and subsequently defines 'us' and 'them'? It would be completely counter-productive. It would create focal points for abuse to be aimed at. It is not the exclusive remit of black players to fight racism, it is for everyone to fight. Would the PFA in its current guise become the White Players' Union? And what if someone suggested the establishment of a White Players' Union? There would be absolute outrage.

I can't but see this suggestion as a slap in the face for our chief executive Gordon Taylor, and everyone who has worked for and with the union over the past three or four decades, to insinuate that they don't care about the issue. The PFA has worked extremely hard on it, and if anyone feels they can be doing more, they should support their union and help make it more effective, not try to split it. Unsurprisingly, the media are going to town over this idea, and quite right too; I couldn't think of anything more absurd.

Fortunately, it was one of those media storms that quickly blew over. A few days later, the circus had moved on. Everybody has distanced themselves from the breakaway initiative and no one is claiming to know much about it or how it started, or who might have wanted it in the first place. As predicted, Jason Roberts stood toe-to-toe with the press and made his position known, but only one other Premier League player stepped forward – behind a press release. With no alternative body for critics to sink their teeth into now, there's only one target left standing: the PFA. I don't mind taking a barrage of questions from Richard Keys, but I must admit I began to lose my patience when a familiar voice added his tuppence to the charade: Monsieur Barton, now plying his trade in France. I cannot catch my breath at the astounding attack he fires at Gordon Taylor, who he described as '[a] fat lazy king so drunk on power he doesn't realise his meal is a rotting mess of maggots'.

This is a guy who has had personal support from Gordon through all of his well-publicised problems. He has needed the PFA to mitigate at Manchester City, Newcastle United and QPR to prevent him getting the sack. How can he have the audacity to call for the head of the head? What is he thinking? There are times when I don't think even Joseph knows.

These have been the most intense weeks of my tenure as chairman of the PFA. I've been averaging between 20 and 25 media/press calls a day for the duration, running about from pillar to post, speaking out, appeasing, justifying, commending, castigating, apologising, lock stock and two smoking 12-bore barrels. Somehow, amid the madness, I've managed to put in my three best performances of the season. What the hell is that all about?

I think that football actually switched its role in my life during this last fortnight. It stopped being the interference that was preventing my progression into the post-football media career that I long for, and actually became a welcome relief from the bombardment of cameras and the continual press intrusion into my and my family's life. Bizarrely, football became enjoyable again because I realised the beauty of it – the opportunity it gives me to make me feel glorious for 90 minutes, even if all hell is breaking loose in the 'real' world. Football is escapism – phenomenally paid, unbelievably enjoyable and incredibly rewarding escapism. Do you know what, there might be two or three years left in these legs! How often do you notice players who are going through well-documented troubles off the field give some of their best performances when you would expect them to be distracted? Now I know why. It's a chance to reconnect with the simple joys of the game that took us into it in the first place.

Sadly, that feeling couldn't extend to my work with the PFA. There was a meeting earlier today that I wasn't able to attend because of my training commitments. A group of current and former black players came in to the union offices to talk through the situation, and it was apparently suggested by some that there was a feeling 'on the ground' that I don't fully represent black players' needs and interests, and that I haven't handled the issue of race adequately enough in my time as chairman.

When the question of why this feeling had arisen was raised, it turned out to stem from an interview I did right at the beginning of the Terry–Ferdinand saga, when I said: 'I hope all parties are innocent.'

This statement was construed as me supporting John Terry directly. Utter crap. I may not have chosen my phrase well, but I can't see anything untoward in hoping that there has not been an incident of racism. We don't want or need it in our game or our society. I would certainly never want anyone found innocent if they are in fact guilty; in that case, I would want them sanctioned in a structured and severe way that serves as punishment, deterrent and re-education of that individual. I conveyed this opinion repeatedly over the entirety of the case and beyond, but it appears to have fallen on deaf ears.

What the hell? Do people think this is an easy job? Actually, they might be right. I don't share the same experiences as this group of players, but ask Darren Byfield who represented him when he was paying for his own treatment and needed support. Ask Steve Kabba who represented him when he needed it. Ask Danny Rose who spoke for him, and who spoke to and supported his dad. Ask Anton Ferdinand who left messages for him and who spoke to his mother at the beginning of all this. Ask Michael Johnson who represented him when he wanted two initiatives pushed forward. Ask Leon McKenzie who spoke up for him in court, supported his missus while he was inside and then helped him present his ideas to the union when he was out. Ask Junior Osborne who helped him when he fell off the football ladder and needed medical attention, and then physiotherapy, for his injury. And don't forget Paul Williams: with the trouble he's having as a coach, who did he turn to?

While you're at it, ask Dean Windass and his wife, David Bell, Drewe Broughton and his wife, Gary Alexander and Joey Barton. Actually, you'd better ask Sasa Curcic who represented him when he needed help, and Vincent Pericard. Oh, and don't forget Irfan Kawri, the scout at Rochdale, the coach Judan Ali and Steven Singh.

The thing is, we have black, white, Asian and overseas members, and it's not possible to understand 100 per cent of their needs either, but I will represent them all to the best of my ability because we are a union. I am willing to listen and learn, and the union is, too. But we can't make the wholesale changes to our set-up that are being dictated by a small percentage of our membership. We can, however, listen to their voices and requests, we can discuss them around the table and make a collective decision on how we move forward. That way we should be able to reach a decision that is in the best interests of us as a whole.

— CHAPTER 12 —

OFFSKI'S STORY

t's the morning of 5 November and the first serious frost of the year. I'm heading to York with Olly Johnson and Dan Parslow, the guys who've kindly let me join their car school even though I don't have a car. It's minus two outside and the heating is on full blast, making it so hot that my nostril hair is melting, my eyes are drier than Jesus's sandals, but I'm still Baltic.

Beep, beep. A text comes through from Melissa Chappell, my media agent, and I spontaneously combust. Woooooo hoooooooo! The news I'd been chasing all summer was finally materialising: ITV want to discuss a working contract to cover the World Cup in Brazil 2014. Happy days! Bouncing up and down in the front seat, I can barely contain my joy. Isn't it sod's law? I hold back from signing football contracts in the hope that something like this will come along, but don't see hide nor hair of it. I swallow my pride, beg for a contract and actually come back round to loving the game once more, and then the golden ticket is waved in front of me. Life is perverse at times, but this is a level of perversion that I can cope with.

Whatever happens, these are merely contract discussions with ITV, and there's nothing concrete on the table as yet, so my future beyond 31 December is still in doubt. All I have is my short-term contract with York City, which expires then, so I need to have a conversation with Gary Mills to see what his plans are. Time passes so quickly during the football season and, consequently, so does a career. It seems that no sooner had I secured employment, and some income to pay the bills, than unemployment was beckoning once more.

The gaffer hasn't mentioned anything about what he intends to do, and I feel a tad apprehensive about asking. It can be a tough situation to judge. I don't want to bowl into his office demanding a contract or a decision, as I am still in a relatively precarious position. I do, however, need clarification on what is to happen in the New Year. If he doesn't want to retain my services, I will have to find a man who does. Fortunately, I do have one thing in my favour: I know that Aidy is interested in taking me back to Northampton. I have to be upfront about this situation, not just to add a little bit of pressure on the gaffer, but also to ensure that I am completely transparent in my actions. I need to act with honesty and integrity at times like this, especially as I'm chairman of the PFA. It wouldn't do for me to get caught up in another scandal.

They say you need to time your run into the box, so after going five games unbeaten I felt this was an opportune moment to discuss my future with the gaffer. We sat in his office at the ground and laid our cards on the table. I outlined how I was appreciative of this opportunity, how I was enjoying being a part of the club and how I feel there is real potential for success this season. I also mentioned that I had been contacted by other interested parties, who were aware that my contract would run out at the end of the year, so I'd prefer to know sooner rather than later whether or not he wanted to keep me on, if that was at all possible. I'm glad I put this information out there, because he already knew. He said he knew that Northampton were interested and wanted to know what they were offering financially. I hadn't talked figures with Aidy at this point, so I said I would find out and let him know.

In one of those coincidences that football often throws up, our next game, on 6 November, was against Northampton. We were loitering in the dressing room waiting for the manager to come in and name the side when a little fracas took place. In such a testosterone-filled environment, there's bound to be a ding-dong or two from time to time. This was the first example of this since I've been at York City. Jamal Fyfield and Jon Challinor ended up Greco-Roman wrestling in the middle of the dressing room over the most trivial of things.

Jam was sitting down reading the match-day programme when Chally came over and slapped it out of his hands and to the floor. It is a regular stunt to pull. If a player ever loses his awareness of what is going on around him, he'll generally end up with his trousers around his ankles, or a doughnut or cake pushed in his face. By sabotaging whatever he is concentrating on, the victim becomes the source of entertainment for the rest of the group. The majority of times the subject of the unwelcome attention accepts his treatment in the way that it is intended, but not always. This was one of those 'not always' moments.

Suitably unimpressed, Jamal picked up an empty dustbin, which was in the centre of the room, and threw it at John with as much force as he could muster from a seated position. Chally caught it and launched it straight back with interest and it bounced off Jam's head with a thunderous echo. Jam exploded from his seat and lunged at Chally, grabbing him by the collar of his tracksuit and trying to throw him to the floor. Chally replied with the same move, grabbing hold of Jam's tracksuit, and an incredibly aggressive do-si-do ensued that was more suited to *Strictly Come Dancing*. Several other players clambered to get in between the scufflers and they were separated with relative ease. The verbals continued across the dressing room.

'Bring it on.'

'Any time.'

'Whatever, whenever.'

'Yeah, well done.'

Like I said, the atmosphere in a football club is similar to a big playground and this is quite typical. It's funny because neither player will ever back down. This was a flash incident, but even if someone gets battered or dominated in a scuffle they will still come out with the bravado at the other end, all to save face and standing in the dressing room.

I've seen plenty of clashes over the years, some complete mismatches and some surprises. When I was at Burnley we had a left-back called Christian Kalvenes, a Norwegian who was an incredibly intelligent guy. He had a really placid demeanour and was one of the quietest people in the world. So much so that he was often perceived to be ignorant by some of the lads and an easy target for banter by others. Robbie Blake is one of the funniest men I have ever met in football. Forever scything people down with witty one-liners, he and Chris Eagles were the hub of all entertainment at the club. Bob would regularly and repeatedly batter Christian verbally, poking fun at one thing or another and pretending to karate chop him in the throat with a shout of 'Sleep'. Christian would just smile and walk on by, or if he was particularly roused, he'd say, 'Well done, Robbie Blakey.'

Nobody ever quite understands how people deal with things like this, but it appears that Christian just suppressed his responses because one day they came flooding out and Bob was to get his comeuppance. A comment from Bob was the final straw and Christian sprinted at him, screaming all sorts of obscenities. He gripped him and threw him to the floor, trying to punch the living daylights out of him. It was only because Bob was a surprisingly good wriggler that he didn't get his backside felt. When they were finally separated, Bob jumped up and started bobbing and weaving, shouting: 'Yeah, you and whose army? Eh?'

Comedy gold.

Bob was the instigator of another one of those incidents that, although intended as a joke, escalated beyond humour. We were at a hotel the night before a match, playing poker to pass the time. Bob and Chris Eagles are two very emotionally volatile people. By that I mean they can swing from happy to sad to angry to elated in seconds and they don't attempt to hide it from you in any way. In fact, they can both dictate the mood of a room or a group of people by their presence, in a positive or negative way according to their choosing. In this game of poker, Bob knocked Chris out of the game with a really lucky river card. Suitably unimpressed, Chris began cursing him, cursing the game, and started to wander over to the settee to watch some TV. To drive the point home about what a terrible beat it was, Bob attacked Chris from behind, bent him over the arm of the settee and began to dry hump him at a ferocious pace.

'Yeah, do you like that? I just nailed you, son.'

We all laughed because we knew that Chris would hate it, but Chris was laughing himself, caught unawares by Bob's speed, strength and technique. Bob carried on pumping away as the laughter died down. And he carried on. And on. And on. He would not stop. Chris started to try to break free, but Bob now had him in a bear hug and was directly on top. Chris's arms were trapped underneath him and he just couldn't get away. The more he struggled the further they slid down and off the settee until they were on the floor. And still Bob carried on. Chris's mood went from humour to annoyance to anger to panic, as he started to shriek under Bob's jackhammer attack. It probably didn't last long, but it certainly seemed it, especially when you're taking a pummelling from the sizeable girth of Robbie Blake. It was only when Bob tired, rolled off panting and sweating, that we saw the reason for Chris's shrieks. He had a huge carpet burn across his cheek and his forehead that was red raw, and he was not amused. There was never a direct repercussion from that event but, knowing Chris as I do, he won't have forgotten it.

These little fights aren't always just between the players, either. I remember a scuffle that I witnessed some years ago, after the team I was playing for had been beaten. The manager was really laying into the squad for our inept performance. He was particularly going to town on our young goalkeeper. Having seemingly had enough of the boss's criticism, he began to get undressed and started to take his shirt off. The manager waited until his keeper had his shirt over his head and then he pounced, throwing a swift one-two and grabbing hold of him. One of our midfielders, an absolute monster of a player, jumped to the keeper's defence, pulling the manager off and making to throw a punch at the gaffer himself. The assistant manager jumped in the way and took a right hand flush in the forehead. It was brilliant.

We helped him up and dusted him off, looking round to see where the gaffer was, and found him hiding under the drinks table. Needless to say, he lost the respect of the dressing room after that. I can appreciate why the senior pros started to be very disrespectful of the manager and dismissive of his words. If you are going to start a fight with your players, at least pick someone with a sizeable frame, reputation and level of standing, not a 19-year-old goalkeeper. And when you start that fight, let him see it coming and don't wait until he's trapped in his own shirt! In those days, that was probably a relatively common incident in football clubs the country over. If a manager so much as laid a finger on a player today, there would be hell to pay. It just wouldn't, and shouldn't, happen any more.

I had a chat with Aidy about what he was offering and the figures ended up being six of one and half a dozen of the other. Northampton were prepared to offer me £1400 per week, with £200 per appearance, for the next 18 months. I relayed this to Gary Mills and he instantly quashed any ideas of matching that.

'We just can't get anywhere near that, Clarke, my budget just won't allow it.'

This was totally understandable and believable. York had only just re-emerged from the Conference. There were still many things about the club that smacked of non-league – like not having lunch after training and having to provide your own drinks for training. The club was making changes, but still had a lot to do and a lot to provide. Gary told me that York could offer me £1000 per week, with £100 per appearance.

The sticking point for me was that this would just be an extension until the end of the season. At 33 years of age, the difference between a six-month contract and an 18-month contract is indescribably huge. I told Gary that I completely understood the budget and accepted the level he was coming in at, but if he could offer me 18 months I would seriously consider staying. Despite the difference in the money, York is less than an hour from my family home, and Mrs C wants us to move to North Yorkshire as all of her family live in Otley, Boston Spa and Burley-in-Wharfedale, so it is geographically perfect.

I went back to Aidy and told him that, although it is not about money, he needed to make it worth my while to move. Now this might sound like a contradiction in terms, but the financial rewards are not the only relevant factor. The offer of an extra £400 per week, £500 if I played, would end up being approximately £300 after tax and National Insurance. This wouldn't even cover the travel costs to get to training and matches all week, so the reality is that we would be financially worse off.

What is even less appealing to me is the amount of time that this would take. I have a young family, my son is settled in his school and my wife finally feels part of a community. I refuse to uproot them again for the sake of 18 months of work. We have had 14 different addresses in the ten years that we have been together. This nomadic existence is not conducive to a settled family life or a stable environment in which your children can grow and develop. I want us to be through with all that. This means I will be yo-yoing up and down the country, on trains initially and then in the car when I get my licence back, to desperately try to steal an hour here or there at home. It's a huge quandary: I have to decide between time with my family and employment security. It's horrible. I keep telling Gem that it's very simple, but it's not. It keeps me awake into the early hours of the morning wondering and analysing: 'Which club will be more successful? Does on-the-pitch success matter at my age? Shall I DEMAND more money? Am I still worth more money?'

Whatever decision I come to, our financial situation won't be drastically affected. My salary from York doesn't cover our monthly expenditure. Even though we slashed our monthly outgoings in the summer from just under £10,000 to just over £4,000, I still have to find at least three paying media commitments each month for us to eat and keep a roof over our heads, and that will have to continue.

I know many of you will be thinking: 'Why don't you downsize and make cutbacks?' But it's not that easy. We sold my car and became a one-car family; we even looked at selling Gem's car, too. However, the contract on that meant that it would cost us to get rid of it, a price we couldn't afford. We have also had our house on the market for over two years now without a single viewing. We were desperate to try to downsize, but it just wasn't possible.

So I wrote down on paper all the factors involved in the two options available to me, and there were two points that stood out. Firstly, although Northampton were below York in the league, I think the potential for success is about equal for both clubs, especially after they destroyed us in the second half at Bootham Crescent with just ten men. I trust

Aidy and I know that he will be amenable to all of my other needs and commitments beyond football. Gary Mills has been very understanding, too, but I often felt like he would much rather I didn't have other things to focus on. Secondly and most importantly, this is a decision between a six-month contract and an 18-month contract. Football is so precarious that I need that security, especially as I have nothing yet signed up with ITV.

My decision has been made. I will still try to get as much money as possible, obviously. I'll ask Aidy for £1600 per week with £200 per appearance, still less than the figure he was offering me five months earlier, and I would commit to signing for him in January.

Well, today was so strange and, if I'm honest, a little emotional. It's 18 November and we had a match away at Port Vale. When we got to the hotel in Stoke to eat our pre-match meal, the gaffer pulled me to one side and asked if I'd spoken to Aidy. I told him I had. In quite an awkward exchange, he asked if I'd come to a decision. It is really difficult to tell a manager that you have decided to leave and, to add insult to injury, for another club in the same division. I felt like I was confessing to an adulterous affair. He asked if Aidy would be willing to do something straight away because, if I had definitely decided to leave, he 'has big decisions to make'. I knew already that Aidy wanted to get me down there as soon as possible, so I was honest.

'Right, then, you know I won't question your commitment and I respect you, but . . .'

And he shook my hand. Thirty minutes later we had the usual team meeting where the manager names the side and gives his big motivational speech. The teamsheet was put up, and I was dropped down to the bench. I can't say I was surprised, but it did smart a bit. Although my mind was made up, it didn't feel as though there was any great attempt to convince me to stay, nor was there going to be any chance of a glorious 'Clarkahimovic' send-off.

Even though I was a sub, and I knew this was to be my last involvement with the squad, I still did everything right. I warmed up professionally and said all the right things to the lads. With ten minutes to go and 2-1 down, GeeBo turned and called me off the bench.

'Get warm. If it gets to two or three minutes to go and we look desperate, you're going on up top.'

I sprinted down the touchline like a classic Eastern European athlete. Excited doesn't even begin to cover it. I could see it now, 92nd minute and the ball is lofted to the back post. CARLISLE . . . YEEEEEESSSS!!!

I've never felt so deflated when my team have scored. Jamie Reed latched on to Smudger's knockdown and the Minstermen were level. I trudged back to the dugout like a schoolboy who'd lost his dinner money. Absolutely gutted. Ho hum, it obviously wasn't meant to be. Back in the dressing room, I looked around at the boys and realised that I was really going to miss these guys. They'd accepted me into the squad instantly and that doesn't always happen. They respected my opinions, abilities and limitations without question and never once made me feel like an outsider who was intruding on their success.

I wondered what it would be that they remembered of me, what my mark would be on their squad? You always want to feel like you've had an impact on a side, like you've brought something to the table that, when you depart, will be a legacy that you leave behind. Well, I can think of three things that might linger on afterwards.

Firstly, the standard of the Mario Kart school has gone through the roof. On coach journeys to away matches, the scope for entertainment has increased dramatically due to the advances of modern technology. Buses now have TV, DVD and Sky Television. The lads have laptops, iPads, iPods, Kindles and hand-held consoles. Some even bring their PS3s on to the bus to play FIFA. Although the classic card school is not dead, it is generally restricted to the older members of the squad. One of the more common activities is Mario Kart on the Nintendo DS. You can have up to eight players racing simultaneously, which is a fantastic way to pass the time. When I arrived I was wiping the floor with everyone, but now the likes of Pottsy, Blairy, Chambo and Kerry were getting competitive. I taught them all the short-cuts and the ability to dodge blue shells, not exactly relevant to the pitch but very relevant to the camaraderie that's formed at the back of the bus.

You may think it's of little importance, but it genuinely keeps some players in high spirits. If you've been dropped from the team, with little hope of getting on the pitch, Mario Kart battles on the away team coach can be a ray of sunshine in a rather lifeless week. There's so much more to it than just the racing, too. You have to give yourself a nickname, which appears onscreen for the others to see. Well, the banter I had with that was infectious. When you realise that the weapons you use are a box, a shell and a banana – oh, the innuendo! Initially I called myself 'Your Mum'. Hilarity ensued with shouts of: 'Who just ate Your Mum's box?'

'Ooooh, I just shelled Your Mum.'

'Your Mum's eating bananas; she's ravenous.'

'Who's on top? Your Mum!'

It's incredibly immature, but the whole working environment of football is. It is barely one or two steps from being in the school playground, and the humour often reflects this. My moniker then progressed to Chairman or Mr Chairman, and on that final trip home from Port Vale I edited my name to Offski.

'Who's Offski?' asked Kerry.

There was a moment's silence before we all fell about laughing as the penny dropped.

The second thing I brought was the mandatory 'Good morning!' greeting and handshake. I never expressed that it was compulsory, but every morning without fail I would greet each player individually with a cheery 'morning' and a handshake or high/low-five of any proportion. I knew it had become engrained when one morning during training Ingy called me over.

'Clarkey, just wanted to ask you something.'

'What's up, fella?'

'Why didn't you say hello this morning?'

'I'm so sorry, Ingy! I must've thought I'd done you already.'

'I was waiting with my hand cocked and everything, and you just walked past.'

'I'm sorry, fella. Take one now. Morning, and have a hug as well.'

You know it's in there when the lads start to do it themselves, and especially when they notice if you miss them out.

Finally, I know that my 'new day' philosophy will stay

with everyone. I came in every day with a smile. Even after that absolute stinker against Coventry, I told them all that shit happens. All you can do is enjoy what today brings. How do I know this? The night of the Port Vale game I received a text and it went like this: 'Your a top man & you make people smile being around them: D x.'

Grammatical error aside, it really warmed my heart to think that this is what I've left with a fantastic group of guys.

To Gary Mills and all the boys at York City, thank you, it's been emotional!

The instantaneous nature of football is something that still catches Mrs C unawares. I returned home from the Port Vale game and told her that the decision had been made, I've told Gary Mills and I'm going to be signing for Northampton.

'Oh, okay. When will you be going down there, then?'

'In the morning.'

'What the hell?!? What happened to January?'

It makes me laugh, but it is a very reasonable response. We were thinking about how we could take five or six weeks to come to terms with the idea of me being away from home. We have arranged to have Christmas at our house this year. All of both our families are invited and I had thought I would finally be able to share a full Christmas Day at home because of the proximity of the football club. Well, all of those plans were shot out of the sky with one decision by a manager, and it pissed Gem right off.

Actually, I think it really upset her more than angered her – everything had to change just because of football. I know that she is fed up with it now and I have almost had my fill, too. She has followed me without question for the past ten years. We have cross-stitched the country virtually every other year. When we arrive at a new club, we generally live in a hotel, then in rented accommodation and then finally buy a property. We are constantly uprooting and moving, not just our personal belongings, but also Gem's work aspirations, social network and any sense of community. Gem has trained and retrained and trained again for various careers to fit in with what's available where we are. She has a degree in broadcasting, started a PGCE, worked in a pub, worked for two years as a volunteer in a teenage mums' drop-in centre, is a qualified masseuse and aromatherapist, has a jewellery business and is now looking at other options around where we may be settling, all in order to insinuate herself into our new surroundings.

Of course, she knew exactly what she was getting into by the time we decided to get married, but that doesn't make it any easier to cope with, nor is that kind of compliance standard procedure. I actually know many players whose wives refuse to leave the comfort of their hometown and family surroundings. I know players whose wives aren't willing to forego their own career aspirations and they move equally as steadfastly in their own direction. I don't want to make this sound like I have placed an expectation on Gem that this is how it should be; I just want to acknowledge that I appreciate how committed and loyal to my career she has been. It is much easier to live like that when it is only the two of you, but now we have two children of our own in tow it is a very different proposition. Fortunately, I suspect this will be my last footballing transfer.

— CHAPTER 13 —

SEEING RED WITH THE COBBLERS

A new day, another new club. Bleary-eyed, I jump on the 05.50 train from Sowerby Bridge to Manchester Victoria. The 50-minute journey is followed by a tram ride to Manchester Piccadilly, where I catch the 07.15 to Milton Keynes. After another 91 minutes on the tracks I make my final connection, the 08.54 to Northampton, which arrives at 09.11. Tickets for the journey and taxis to and from the stations see me £100 lighter and that's four hours of my life I'll never get back. I cannot do this every day. Travel weariness aside, it would be the equivalent of losing a whole working day, every day. With all the roles that I'm currently juggling, it would be a monumental loss of time.

Even though I'm going back to a club that I was at no more than six months ago, I still have a lot of anxiety and apprehension coursing through my body. When I joined Northampton in January 2012, they were bottom of League 2 and in a world of trouble. The pressure on me was diminished somewhat as their situation really couldn't get any worse. If I had an impact, it could only be a positive one and it was likely to be recognised. If I failed to make an impact and their situation didn't change, then I wouldn't be held accountable as the position was already established.

The situation today is an entirely different proposition as Northampton are perched mid-table in League 2. Which means that I could have a positive impact and help the team climb up the table, but I could equally have a negative impact that sees the team tumble down. The fact that last season did end 'successfully', with us climbing up to 20th, also means that there will be added expectations of me. What fate will befall us this time?

I have to admit that arriving at Sixfields felt good. The familiarity of the ground, the people working in the offices and my old gaffer immediately put me at ease. There is still a lot of business to sort out, as we haven't yet clarified the terms of the permanent contract that I am to sign. I was advised to ensure that it was all set out in writing before I even considered getting on a train. The safest way to think of it is thus: football clubs are not to be trusted; managers are not to be trusted; and chairmen are not to be trusted. I know it's a really paranoid and cynical view of the football world, but it prevails for good reason. I have seen numerous situations where agreements and promises have been reneged on, even when they are in writing.

However, I have a level of trust and respect for Aidy Boothroyd that I hope is well placed. My immediate future is very simple: to play for Northampton at once, I have to sign on loan. This means that the club will simply take over the terms of my current contract until it expires on 31 December. There can be no salary adjustment or improvement; everything stays exactly the same. What this actually means is that I will immediately be financially worse off due to the costs of travel and accommodation, but hopefully I can get the club to contribute towards those. What happens beyond then is still up in the air.

Aidy and I greet each other with a big smile and a bigger hug; it's good to be back. He tells me that the chairman is playing silly buggers. The £1600 per week + £200 appearance money that I've asked for is impossible, as he's been told there's no chance of my getting that, but he was sure he would get Mr Cardoza to agree to £1400 + £200. That's good enough for me. I've got five weeks to do my part and show the chairman that I'm worth it, although he should be well aware of this from last season, and I'm confident I will do that.

I breezed into the dressing rooms with a few whoops and jeers from the lads. Handshakes and man-hugs abounded as I reacquainted myself with my old team-mates and introduced myself to the new acquisitions.

'That's a fine,' was the first thing Kelvin Langmead greeted me with, along with a huge grin of satisfaction. The skipper was showing me absolutely zero mercy. Apparently, we have to be in at 9am for training, and it is a £25 fine for anybody who fails to adhere to this, newbies included. I may have to take this one to court because I haven't signed any papers yet, so I'm not officially under Kelv's jurisdiction. I can't have this day costing me any more than it has done already, but I go along with the banter for the time being.

'Yes, Celeb, what's happening?'

Turning round I am enveloped in the Kodiak bear-like grip of Adebayo Akinfenwa, or Bayo as he's known, and we dance the man-hug tango around the dressing room. His pet name for me was coined the season before, when one week he saw more of me on the TV than he did at work. I cannot exaggerate how much love I have got for this guy. B is one continual surprise. Firstly, he is an absolute colossus of a man. I haven't seen a physique like his since I played alongside Danny Shittu at QPR and Watford. It defies the laws of physics that he can play football at all, let alone with the amount of pace and quality that he does.

Witnessing this at close quarters was a sight to behold. He is so strong that when he decides that you are staying where you are, you are staying exactly where you are. Then he dumbfounds you with a turn of pace that should not be possible for a being of his size. When the ball finally arrives, he has a deftness of touch that is just too good for defenders in League 2 to deal with, and most probably those higher up would struggle, too.

Secondly, the love and generosity of this man away from the pitch completely belies his 'Beast Mode' persona. He shows a level of passion that makes him an extremely emotional person. I would hate to be the person on the receiving end of his explosive anger, but there would be little doubt that that person will have pretty much deserved such a response. However, to those inside his circle of trust, he will display a loyalty that would see him walk to the ends of the earth.

Finally, there is a depth of thought and a level of intellect that has seen us chat for many, many hours. B speaks with a vocabulary that contains so much slang that I often have to get him to break it down for me, but then he is the same with some of the vocabulary that I use. If you happened to be sitting behind us in Starbucks (or any other hot beverage establishment), you could be forgiven for thinking that we were speaking different languages. Amazing then that there are so many similarities in our life experiences and philosophy.

'Welcome home, my general!'

Yes, I made the right choice.

For the second year in a row, I was making my second debut in the same season, and this was my second debut for Northampton Town, if such a thing is possible. Having played with the majority of the same squad last year, I was feeling very relaxed about it until Aidy named me as the left-sided centre-half. I am used to playing on the right side of the two centre-halves and have done so for the majority of my career. Moving me approximately 20 yards to the left makes a massive difference to my game.

Defensive positions are pretty much second nature to me now. Wherever the ball is on the pitch, I instinctively know where to be after 17 years of repetition in matches and training. Now it will be like playing a mirror image of the game I am used to and that will take a lot of conscious thought. Having to assess where you are standing on a pitch, where you need to go next and whether that is all correct can mean that you make decisions and execute the actions a second or two later than you normally would. In football terms, that can be a difference of three to five yards, which is a very long way. Playing on the left side also means that I will be approaching clearances and passes on my left foot the majority of the time. I am barely competent on my right foot with any degree of accuracy, but my left foot is for standing on. It is absurd the amount of doubt I have in my mind when I am trying to strike the ball with my left foot. I know all about the power of positive thinking and so I repeatedly tell myself that I can do it.

'Just do it, just feed the ball into the striker.' SHANK.

'Okay, the next one will be fine. Don't try and kick it too hard – just relax.' SHANK.

'Please don't shank it, please don't shank it, please, please, please!' SUPER SHANK.

These fears are compounded by the groans that emanate from the stands after each wayward effort, culminating in the ironic cheer when you finally get one right. There is so much shame and embarrassment when it gets to this point. The shame is in the fact that you are a professional foot-baller and you can't even kick the ball. The embarrassment is because thousands of people are watching; they have seen every one of your terrible efforts and you'll probably be the source of their ire or amusement for the rest of the day.

The only solution to having a sub-standard left foot is to take the ball across on to your right foot and kick it with that. This brings its own problems, though. Again, it can cost you time to take the extra touch necessary, and you are moving the ball infield, towards your opponent, which closes down your own space, and this is counter-productive. Just to make the whole situation more precarious, if you make a mistake moving on to your right foot, then you are likely to put your opponent straight through on goal. If I'm playing right centre-half and do the same thing, I'll be giving the ball away on the outside, which generally gives me an opportunity to recover as my opponent doesn't have a clear run on goal, so this is much the better scenario. I'm going to have to summon all my powers of positive thinking to get me ready for this game. The level of expectation surrounding my arrival is fantastic for my ego, but just about as much as my nerves can handle.

A comprehensive 3-0 defeat of Accrington Stanley has alleviated my fears somewhat. I must admit that it had more to do with the performance of my centre-half partner and skipper Kelvin Langmead than my own display. He is a completely different animal to the one I played alongside last season. Physically he looks fitter and stronger, mentally he seems far more assured and self-confident and, in the context of leadership, he was commanding and authoritative. He rescued me after three errors tonight and did so without complaint or redress. I can happily play next to that week in, week out.

The change in Kelvin has caused me to reassess my standing within the dressing room. As a team player, you have to make sure that you conform to the established hierarchy. If I don't behave in a subservient way to the captain, this would only undermine the regime and severely upset the dynamic in the dressing room. That being said, I still want to see whether I still have respect around the club and what level it is at. It may sound bizarre, but as much as I respect Aidy and Kelv, I feel I need to see where I stand. Just like a kid, I want to push the limits to see where the boundary is.

I got my opportunity in the first training session after the game, which is when we usually do 'activation' (a series of exercises and stretches that warm up the muscles ready for football-specific training) and then go over to the gym to do a bike and pool session. I knew that I wanted to leave straight afterwards, so that I could start the four-hour journey home as soon as possible, so I called my own meeting with the boss to discuss my diary while the boys all shot off to the gym. While we were talking, a text came through from Craig, the fitness coach, asking where I was. I didn't reply, but continued sorting out my diary with the gaffer. When we had finished, I rocked up to the gym and strolled in, then began to stroll straight out again as I headed off for the train station. Craig immediately appealed to Kelv about whether this was acceptable or not. Unbeknown to them, I was actually awaiting the reaction with bated breath. It's a new dynamic in the club, with Kelv as skipper, and I can see he has stepped up to the plate. However, I also heard one or two comments along the lines of 'CC is above the system' or 'Mr Chairman plays by his own rules'. I wonder if I can get away with this.

It appears that I can. Kelv just shrugged his shoulders and carried on with the session. Bouncing to my own beat feels good, but the truth is that I won't take the piss. If you have established a senior position in the squad, you can actually utilise it for a very powerful purpose. When things need to be done or changes need to be made, if I take a lead on such matters, it can hopefully cause other lads to think: 'Okay, if Clarke is doing this or going there then I should too.'

There is so much psychology within a team scenario, but you must assert a role where your moves have an impact. The flipside is that this position can be abused. That is where the manager comes in. He must clearly define what is acceptable and what is not. By doing that, he forges the working environment, and he must use the strong characters within the team to endorse the values by which he wants to lead the team.

My ankle seems to just randomly lock at the moment. There's no swelling or anything in there, but suddenly it will refuse to move and cause me substantial pain when it does so. I know that footballers' ankles are notorious for the wear and tear they suffer, and mine have seen a significant amount of trauma over the last 20 years, since I was a teenager. It wouldn't surprise me if there was a high level of degeneration in them. But there is a part of me that is scared to find out. I really don't want to hear that they have deteriorated so much that playing isn't advisable, which is why I am very apprehensive about getting them checked out. But there is another part of me that knows I can't keep something like this to myself forever.

It has occasionally happened in games that my ankle jars and causes a shooting pain through the joint, but then it will free up again after a couple of minutes' hobbling. It could well be that there are some osteophytes floating around in there that are just jamming in the joint from time to time, so I should get my ankles x-rayed. Our two coaches here at the Cobblers, Tim Flowers and Andy King, have barely got a working joint between them. They hobble around between sessions like they've been cast in iron limbs.

I don't want to push my body to the extent where I won't be able to run around with my kids in five years' time. Many ex-footballers tell me to play as long as I possibly can, because 'you're a long time retired'. This is very true, but surely it is a more enjoyable retirement when you have full use of your limbs? I suspect another reason some players say this is because they still hanker after being in the game when they do retire, and usually end up as scouts, coaches and managers.

I'm not in the same position. I have a real desire to go into broadcasting when I finish. The thought of doing so fills my belly with a similar fire to the one I had about football when I started my career. Surely retirement is not as long when you are moving on to something else that gets your juices flowing? But I mustn't get ahead of myself: I need to get that future career path sorted, but in the meantime I must make sure my body is up to my current job.

A trip to Oxford was next on the fixture list in what is viewed as our local derby. It was a game that would bring about a very testing situation. The 2-1 defeat was compounded in the 89th minute when I received a second booking and trudged back to the dressing room for an early shower. I have been sent off ten times in my career, and each time I have felt a level of remorse and guilt that is only enhanced when my team-mates join me after the final whistle. Fortunately, in this instance, there was also a degree of understanding and support from them, which somewhat mitigated my mood. Being chairman of the PFA, on the other hand, means that the ignominy of it all, as far as the wider world is concerned, is increased. That being said, I wasn't prepared for the deluge of abuse that ensued.

I was astonished to find that my Twitter feed was filled with cries of 'disgrace', 'hypocrite' and 'fucking gobshite'. A tad harsh, I thought, until I realised it had been reported that I was sent off for foul and abusive language. The truth of it was that my first booking came when their big striker, James Constable, got in front of me and would have been through on goal. I gave his shirt a couple of tugs so that he didn't break clean through. It was a cynical foul, one that is called a 'good foul' when you get back in the dressing room. In those circumstances, I'd definitely rather take one for the team than let a striker get a free shot. It gave us the chance to get our defensive line set up so we could defend the free-kick, which was a far more advantageous position for us.

The only drawback to picking up a yellow card was that I knew I couldn't really touch or tackle anyone for the remainder of the game in anything other than a perfect manner. Well, I didn't manage that. First of all, I shanked a clearance off Constable's back and he got to the ricochet first. Alfie Potter then overlapped him, looking to get into the space behind me. I had to back off and start to head towards the space. At this point, the attacking team had all the cards in their hand. Constable can just stride forward into the space that I'm vacating, picking a pass or taking a shot. While he is in front of us this is okay. My concern has to be the runner. If he gets the ball at his feet, running in behind our defensive line, then we are extremely vulnerable.

When defenders and attackers are both running towards the goal, a ball whipped across with pace can be slotted home by anyone. I started to back off in front of Potter, but he still had the advantage as he was facing the direction he wanted to go. Should the pass be played to him, I would need to turn 180 degrees and then accelerate to catch or beat him to the ball.

As good strikers should, Constable slid the ball into the space for his winger and I turned to start the chase. I'd actually turned in front of Potter, but he was already going much quicker than me and would easily have beaten me to the ball, so I stepped into his line to make him run further. He ran straight into the back of me and fell to the ground. If it had happened at the other end, I'd have been asking for a free-kick, as I would argue that someone can't expect to run through you to get to the ball. Equally, in a defensive situation, I don't think I should have to get out of the way just because my opponent is quicker. Sadly, the referee viewed it differently and went straight to his pocket. I knew I was off, so I jogged straight down the tunnel without a word being said.

You may ask why I should feel upset that my dismissal was reported as being for foul and abusive language; after all, footballers are renowned for their coarse and crude language on the pitch. The problem was that I'd been campaigning strongly and openly for our industry to clamp down on the language players use on the pitch, and have frequently lambasted colleagues for their lack of verbal control, which was why this had such great potential for embarrassment. It is often said that bad language is part of the culture or used in the heat of the moment, but I believe they are excuses, and bad ones at that. It's only a part of the culture because we allow it to pass unpunished on a daily and weekly basis, and that's what our kids are watching and learning. I believe we can change this.

Desperate to find the source of this misinformation, I put out a tweet of correction and asked who had said such a thing. Short of Sally Bercow (though she was suggested), the answer was everyone. Each of the major outlets for Saturday football, the BBC, Sky Sports News, 5 Live and talkSPORT, had relayed this lie to the masses. Even my mate Jeff Stelling had a chuckle at the irony of the situation.

As I filtered through the replies, it transpired that it was the original Press Association feed from the game that had stated I'd been guilty of foul and abusive language, and this turned out to be the source that all the other outlets use.

The PA apparently have a person at every match who relays the events in real-time down the line to someone who then broadcasts them across a universal feed. Anyone who was present at the game couldn't possibly have been 'mistaken' about the reason why I was sent off, so I felt sure that someone had opted to play silly buggers with me.

Thank God for social media. By targeting known folk at all the networks, corrections were made on Sky Sports News, *The Football League Show*, 606 on 5 Live, and talkSPORT's Twitter feed. By 9pm, I had a written apology from the Press Association. How times have changed. No more stewing for days or weeks while I try to straighten out the mess. A few button taps and the charge was batted out of the park. The Press Association stated that it was 'a casual error'. I'm not sure that's a viable defence in a defamation case, which would be the usual path after the character assassination that followed, but we don't need to go there.

This situation did show me that, just like the over-zealous passing of wind, trials by Twitter can leave marks that are very hard to remove. For every one of those who back-tracked, there was an equivalent number who resorted to saying 'so that makes it all right then' or 'abusive language or physically harming your fellow members, surely that's worse?' It made me realise that the instant nature of social media can back people into a corner. Even though it had helped me to correct the initial mistake almost instantly, some of those who had judged me and commented felt obliged to maintain some form of attack instead of conceding that they had spoken too soon.

And this is how mud sticks.

Hastily assembled and globally published opinion is

causing people to 'find' a reason to continue their vein of thought, rather than face the humiliation of backtracking. And so, trial by Twitter is held in Kangaroo Court. Once something gets in the system and is anywhere near viral, the damage is done. Even if all attempts at correction reach the previously affected audience, the stance of some will not be moved. Humans are impulsive, judgemental and proud. Controlling these emotions is the difference between responsible and reckless use of social media. Let's hope that technological advances don't reach the court-rooms, because an online jury would see our conviction rates go through the roof.

CHAPTER 14

SNORT THE PORT AND BEYOND

There are many ways in which football clubs differ, but if there is one thing that is identical the nation over it's the lads' night out. It is an event that is almost exclusive to British football, and the influx of overseas players has seen the frequency of these occasions dwindle somewhat, but it is still very much a part of the game. Whether it is in the guise of a team-bonding session, a pre- or post-season tour, a match celebration or drowning sorrows after a defeat, they all come down to the same thing: a free-for-all night of drinking and debauchery.

Just as with any other workplace, the Christmas party is the main event of the year and warrants meticulous planning. It has usually been a topic of conversation since September and someone will have been nominated to make all the necessary arrangements. It is a lot harder than you may think to get an establishment to welcome a party of 30 men, usually in fancy dress, whether we're footballers or not. In actual fact, we often have to pay over the odds, not because as footballers we have the means to afford it, but because we have a reputation for causing more problems than it's worth. And for very good reason.

The boys at York were planning their weekend jaunt the week before I left. They called a meeting to lay down the ground rules for the trip to Newcastle as follows:

- Compulsory attendance on Saturday and Sunday
- Compulsory fancy dress on the Sunday
- Must meet in the hotel lobby at midday Sunday
- No one is allowed to leave before 3pm Sunday
- No one is allowed to change their fancy dress outfit before 3pm Sunday
- No show is £250 fine

I put my hand up and asked whether being an alcoholic was grounds for mitigation on the fine. After a slight pause, everybody burst into laughter. The best way to defuse uncomfortable situations is just to deal with them directly. If you can add a bit of humour, then so much the better. I clarified that I was being serious, and the skipper asked if it would be all right for me to be there at all. I explained that I didn't want to risk it, because I know myself and if I capitulate and start drinking with them, with a full weekend's disco pass, it would be a one-way ticket to Doolallysville, Tennessee.

When I arrived at Northampton, they were in the middle of the same process, and I have asked to withdraw from their plans as well, even though it is a group of guys who I know and trust.

The truth about situations like this is that I would dearly love to join the guys for a weekend of fun and banter, but I just can't trust myself. I would head out with the best of intentions, either to have only a couple or even not to drink at all, but once the party got going I would have to confront 'the voice'. Oh yes, the very same voice that drives me to succeed, that makes every run or session of paramount importance and a chance to prove myself, the one that makes me push myself to the limit even on easy jogs. It's that same voice that tells me: 'These guys have never seen you drink! I bet they don't believe anything they've heard about you. I bet they think they can drink you under the table, and they'll never know because you've shit out.'

And then it's on. I *have* to show them that I can drink copious amounts of alcohol, levels that they've never seen before and, once it starts, I just don't want it to stop. I will pinball from one establishment to the next, in desperate need of more alcohol to push the boundaries even further. I know that it is so irrational, so ridiculous, so illogical, but even though I know that this is what will happen, it can be a real conscious struggle to opt out on certain occasions. Alcohol is a very cunning drug. It lulls me into a false sense of security. After a period of abstinence, I may well go for a meal with Mrs C and have a glass of wine. All of a sudden my brain is telling me that I've won. This is it, I have conquered the demon that lies within, and I am no longer a slave to the juice of Zeus! So what do I do? I decide it's time to celebrate and I can get royally wankered because it doesn't matter any more, as I'm cured! And so it begins again . . .

My personal drinking habits were formed long before I got into football. They could provide enough material for a whole book on their own but, in order to put you in the picture, I'll try to give a brief insight into where my sordid affair with alcohol took me. My friends were regularly smoking weed and drinking every weekend from around the age of 13. They would all gather at the local park, Blue Bridge on Bent Lane, and doss the hours away with a few spliffs and several bottles of Ye Olde English Cider, Mad Dog 20/20, Thunderbirds or something equally cheap and potent.

My parents were really strict and would never let me stay out beyond 8.30 or 9pm, which caused me huge problems. There was no way I could get smashed with everyone else, not unless I started at about four o'clock and gave myself enough time to drink, fall over, sober up and get home. So what tended to happen was that I didn't go out unless I had the opportunity to really go for it. This would be either when I knew Mum and Dad were going out, so they would be home late, or I concocted a story that I was 'camping out' in someone's back garden or the bluebell woods or somewhere. Once I had the licence to get drunk, I went hell for leather. Even at such an early age I would drink until I passed out, or drink to 'blackout' where I would have zero recollection of what went on the night before.

When I left home at 16 and moved into digs in Blackpool, my drinking became a far more structured affair. Going out on a Saturday night was very much the norm. Win or lose, hit the booze; if you draw, hit it more. In those days, the management and staff at football clubs were much more relaxed about this sort of thing; indeed, it was virtually expected for all players to be doing it. As long as it was being done at the right time, with no signs of anyone getting into trouble, it was acceptable and seen as a good way for players to let off a bit of steam. Even when someone was getting into trouble, if they were producing the goods on a Saturday then a blind eye was often turned.

I revelled in this environment. Being released from the shackles of a very disciplined home, I ran around Blackpool like a kid in a sweet shop. Still in my teens, I stayed with the safety of my team-mates at this time, hitting the same circuit of Never On A Sunday and then Main Street/Bizness every Saturday. Jamie Cross, Simon Seaton, Jason Jarrett and Steve Longworth were my usual crew.

But it wasn't long before I started hitching a night out midweek with some of the older pros. This was far more dangerous territory. The midweek nights out were almost reserved as a privilege for the senior players, as though they had earned the extra night of fun. So when I ventured out with the likes of Lee Thorpe, John Hooks and Scott Darton to Brannigans and The Cotton Club, it was a much more clandestine affair. They would probably be okay if the manager found out, as they were in their early twenties. A 17-year-old rookie like me probably wouldn't be, and that proved to be the case.

In a small town such as Blackpool, which had such a transient population depending on the season, the drinking circuit was full of the same faces in the same places. As members of the local football team, the vast majority of proprietors knew exactly who we were. So when it was reported to our manager, Gary Megson, that I had been out drinking after a reserve team game, there was little I could offer by way of defence. His reaction was to teach me a lesson and make sure it served as an example to the other young lads that this was unacceptable behaviour.

For two weeks I had to report to the training ground at 9am, get changed into my kit and start running around the perimeter of Squire's Gate. I wasn't allowed to stop until everyone had finished the morning session, usually around three hours later. I then had to get all of the training gear in by myself, grab a quick sandwich and report to the gym at 1pm. The remainder of the day was spent on the rowing machine, non-stop for the entirety of the afternoon session, probably another two or three hours. It was absolute torture. But it taught me an incredibly important lesson: don't get caught.

I found that throughout my formative years, getting caught and punished never really made me contrite; it made me cleverer about how I was going to do something the next time. And this pattern of behaviour continued. I didn't stop going out midweek, I just went to more low-key places and with people who weren't so well known (in the context of 'local celebrity') in order to be more discreet.

My transfer to QPR gave me all of the necessary ingredients for a successful drinking life. The anonymity afforded to a young mixed-race man in London was awesome, and this, coupled with a new-found wealth, meant any night and virtually any place could be party time. The lads I joined there had a totally different standard of drinking, one I had not encountered before – it was Dane Bowers 'Another Level'.

We went to the south coast for our pre-season tour and were allowed out for one night by the gaffer, Gerry Francis. I was introduced to one of the most mind-blowing drinking games I have ever played: 'Snort the Port'. Random rules were made up, so that you were not able to point with your finger, or you had to use certain names for people and you weren't allowed to cuss. The forfeit for committing any of these offences was to snort a teaspoon of port. My good God!

Needless to say, I was absolutely paralytic after an hour and the rest of the night is completely blank. I woke up in a piss-soaked bed, a dead cert whenever I drank (so much so that Mrs C used to get me to sleep in the bath if I'd been out), no clothes, no money and no memory. None of the lads enlightened me either; they just chuckled about how it was a 'great night' and I was a 'good lad'. At every club I've played for there has been an inextricable link between alcohol consumption and level of esteem. If you ever hear footballers talking about a former colleague or a footballing friend and they say 'he's a great lad', it will almost always be followed by the line 'loves a drink'.

There has been a slight shift in football clubs in recent years as players have become much more aware of their diet and the amount they drink, but I would say that, on the whole, this attitude still prevails.

My drinking was still strictly Saturday to Tuesday when I first arrived at QPR, but that all changed with my knee injury. The combination of pain, fear and boredom was a recipe for disaster. I spent so much time in my flat by myself, and getting drunk was one of the only ways to pass the hours that I could come up with. I think there was a part of me that was enjoying the opportunity to get wasted every day, and it was so easy. I could phone in for a delivery of alcohol, and then begin to work my way through it. I would inevitably hobble across the road to the bookies for some light entertainment, then hobble back via the 7-Eleven to restock my wine or smokes or both. No one could make me toe the line for two reasons: firstly, I was very isolated and didn't really show people the extent of my behaviour, and secondly, if anyone did say anything, I would just ignore them.

Although this period culminated in my suicide attempt, that wasn't the moment I realised I had a drinking problem. After I was released from hospital, Racheal and her family kept me much closer to home, with a far keener eye on what

I was up to. As my knee started to improve and it seemed that I might actually be able to return to football, I started to cut back on my drinking. In actual fact, I didn't drink for around seven months prior to returning to the first team at QPR, a target that had been set by Racheal and Prav in order to give me the best chance of doing so. However, when I did finally get back into action, I got straight back into the socialising action too, but still stayed within the reasonable parameters of drinking just between Saturday and Tuesday.

My descent into uncontrollable and destructive drinking started with an external trigger. It was the Division 2 play-off final for QPR against Cardiff at the Millennium Stadium, Cardiff, on 25 May 2003. As you can imagine, playing Cardiff in Cardiff, in a game of such magnitude, meant that the atmosphere was, well, Dane Bowers. It was like nothing I had experienced in my life. The noise, the size of the stadium, the amount of people and the prize at stake – this was the biggest and most important game of my career so far, and I knew it. I was nervous because Robert Earnshaw had scored a hat-trick against us earlier in the season, and it was the first time that Gemma (the future Mrs C but we didn't know it yet) had come to watch me play. I had told her previously that I played football, but she thought I meant on a Sunday, for fun, so when I invited her to come and watch she wasn't all that enthused.

We played in an all-white kit that day, still my favourite-ever club strip, and it was all going to plan when Earnshaw got subbed off in the 79th minute. It was still 0-0 and I thought we would go on and win the game. His replacement, however, had other ideas. Andy Campbell popped up in the second half of extra time with a cheeky lob over our keeper, Chris Day, and our dreams were shattered. I collapsed at the final whistle and wept. I wept in the dressing room and at the hotel. I wept continually until a glorious moment, the moment I got drunk. The alcohol was like a general anaesthetic; it took all of the hurt and regret and emotion away from me, and I loved it. Although there had been a crowd of more than 66,000 there, I still don't think Gem completely understood the significance of the game, because she asked me in the hotel afterwards: 'Why were you crying on the pitch? It was a bit embarrassing!'

No sympathy there, then. Gem had no comprehension of football and the importance of it to me as a player, or even to a football fan. She grew up in a house that had zero interest in the game, and this was her first foray into my world. I wonder if she ever rues the fateful day. I drank some more. I started to move beyond numb and into a completely different zone. I liked this zone. It was one that made me feel as though I didn't care if she's embarrassed about me, because I was going to get Gem and make her my woman. The next day all of the negative feelings came rushing back, and they brought with them a few more: sadness, loss, embarrassment, shame, guilt and failure. I needed to get away from these feelings, and fast. My elixir wasn't far away.

As soon as we returned to Shepherd's Bush I got straight on the sauce. It covered me in a cloak of invincibility, in a place where I could not be harmed because I didn't give a flying fuck. It was awesome. I didn't want to take this cloak off, not ever, so I drank for the entirety of the summer 2003. To say that those five or six weeks are hazy would be a lie. For something to be hazy, it implies that you have sight of it but it is out of focus or blurred. I have *zero* recollection. I could not tell you where I went, what happened, with whom or why. All I remember doing is leaving my house with my wallet and my passport, just in case.

I somehow reported back to training on time and started to get back into the regime of professional sport. This was when the second event occurred which, coupled with the rapacious appetite that I had acquired over the summer, gave me the internal trigger to lose control. My best friend from school, Andy Jones, had been medically discharged from the Paras due to sciatica and he was now looking for somewhere to live. By now, I had of course split up with Racheal and I wanted to move out of the place that we had rented together. So Andy and I shacked up in the perfect bachelor pad in Chiswick. We had decided to take the property before we even saw it, purely because it was on Beavor Grove. Number 2 Beavor Grove – it was an awesome address for two young men on the prowl.

In order to celebrate, we decided to go out every night for two weeks. It was early pre-season, so as long as I was still putting in the work the next day then I felt it wouldn't matter too much. Andy didn't yet have a job, so we met early afternoon every day at the Hart. We would then proceed to drink until closing, whereon we would head into the West End until the early hours. I must have built a huge tolerance level in the summer, because I found that I could drink copious amounts of alcohol: pints, shots, cocktails, always culminating in a bottle or two of fizz – I could put the lot away. What was a new discovery was that I could do that and still train the next day. I thought I really was invincible.

My group of friends at this time weren't other footballers. I had learnt by now that in order to maintain a level of privacy (or secrecy), I had to socialise outside of football circles. I had struck up a friendship with three other guys who lived together. They were an actor, a radio producer and a band manager and, between the five of us, we could pretty much get into most places in town. It was with these guys that the second trigger came.

The actor, Ralf Little, was a very self-assured guy. Everything had an element of competition, whether it was drinking, dancing, women, Pro-Evolution Soccer, income, level of fame, *everything*. This triggered two things within me. Firstly, I wanted to be liked by all of these guys. This meant that I would say yes to everything. If there was a party I was there, a drink to be had I was there, an event to be seen at I was there. I wanted to be a part of the group. Secondly, I wanted to win. This may sound pathetic, but it is where I was at. I wanted to be cooler, I wanted to party harder, I wanted to be richer (or look richer if I wasn't), I wanted to impress him and everyone around us. He would often say that I shouldn't really be going out. He was desperate to be a footballer and genuinely believed that he was good enough. He even came for training at the club one day for a programme he was doing and, I must say, he didn't look out of place. Knowing that I had something he wanted fuelled my actions. In my head, I convinced myself that if I could show him that I could live his lifestyle and still be a footballer then that would set me apart, that would mean I win. What an idiot.

As I continued to party, two nights per week became three, which became four, which became five. The only restriction I had was that I would never go out the night before a game. I started to find that I would arrive at work in a complete state. I would stumble through training, running off as much ale as I could from the night before and then, after a shower, I felt magnificent. I was ready to go again, straight from training to the Hart. This was usually at the beginning of lunchtime. Andy had found a job by now, so I had to wait until he finished at five. I would sit in the pub on my own and play pool against strangers for pints of Hoegaarden. I was very good, but remarkably better with several pints inside me; Bill Werbeniuk had nothing on me.

By the time Andy arrived, I was usually at least ten pints deep (always with Amaretto chasers) and had accrued some new 'friends'. I would buy round after round of cocktails and shots to get people to come and drink with me. It was so pitiful. I had an American Express charge card, which I would put behind the bar wherever we went. It was limitless, so I would never run out of money. I just had to make sure I cleared it at the end of the month. It got to the point where my salary wasn't covering the AmEx bill, even though I only ever used the card for drinking. When I did eventually go into the clinic my local was devastated. Their income for the week went down by over 30 per cent. That's ridiculous, yet it's still something I have a warped sense of pride about. It is this 'winning' mentality: 'Yeah, I fucked up, and I fucked up bigger than anyone can imagine.' I can't pretend it's not in there; it's a part of my crazy thought process.

It all came to a head when I turned up for the team coach one day absolutely stinking of booze. As soon as the manager, Ian Holloway, got on the bus he could smell me. Knowing exactly who it was, he gripped me by the collar and said: 'What the hell are you playing at?'

'Trying to get some sleep,' was my terrible attempt to allay the situation. Olly literally threw me off the bus and told me to train with the youth team for the next two days while they were away. I trained with the kids that morning and then, you guessed it, went straight down the pub. I got obliterated and then, instead of turning up for training with the kids the next day, I went to Yates's at opening time and drank a bottle of wine with a straw. I moved on to a bar with *Soccer Saturday* on the TV, ordered a pint and sat and watched for the updates on the vidiprinter.

This was my moment. They say that every recovering addict has one, their rock bottom. Well, this was mine. I was on my own, sitting in a bar, watching for the result of the team *that I play for* to come on the box. What the hell am I doing? Millions of people would chop their fingers off to be in my position. Hell, I would have done many years before. Why was I throwing it away just to go out and get drunk? I didn't know the answer. I walked back to the house and phoned Olly on the way. I told him that I needed help and I didn't know what to do.

Olly was awesome. He took me round to his house and I had dinner with his wonderful family. We sat and talked for hours and I cried and cried. Olly said that he didn't know what to do or how to 'fix' me, but he was damn sure he could find someone who could. This was where the Sporting Chance clinic in Liphook, James West and Peter Kay entered my life. I cannot exaggerate the importance of this in my life. I didn't know it, but Olly was making the necessary arrangements to sack me when I called him. If that had happened, I can't even begin to imagine where I would have ended up. My shame and embarrassment had already taken me to where I was; the utter humiliation of being sacked would have been like dropping a Mentos in a bottle of Coke

– I would have exploded in complete self-destruction. Knowing the situations I had already gotten myself into through drink, I genuinely believe I would be dead now had I not called out to Olly and had he not supported me. I am eternally grateful to him for this.

Sporting Chance was amazing. I had one-to-one counselling sessions with James and Peter that just stripped my psyche and my emotions bare. Trawling through my thought processes was a disgusting procedure. It was shameful, hurtful, embarrassing, enlightening and liberating. The journey to becoming self-aware was an arduous one, but it helped me discover why I acted and reacted the way I do.

The next job was to learn ways to address those actions and adjust the reactions, to create new synapse circuits that would spark a different response to my emotional triggers. I went through the 28-day period and emerged the other side with a very different approach to life.

I have to thank the people who guided and supported me through it. It started with Ian Holloway; without his compassion for my situation and magnanimous approach to the solution, I wouldn't have had the opportunity to begin any sort of recovery. The football club were equally as supportive. They could quite easily have made an executive decision about my future, but Nick Blackburn and the other board members trusted Olly's judgement and supported my journey. The QPR fans were awesome. They set up a website on which messages of support and good wishes were posted. I still have the print-out of every single message in my house to this day. I will never forget them. It was the first time I witnessed the community nature of a football club. The PFA and Gordon Taylor were by my side all the way, in the way of financial support by funding my place at the clinic, and emotional support in the constant contact afterwards. My family, although shocked, were constantly thinking of and praying for me, surrounding me with the love and counsel that are of paramount importance at a time like this.

The two people who stand front and centre, though, are Peter Kay and the future Mrs C. Peter (or Chef, as he is affectionately known) transcended counselling with me. We had an instant connection of mind and soul that has made him a close and lifelong friend and someone in whom I place 100 per cent of my trust. I love you, Chef! Gem and I had barely started seeing each other prior to my going in the clinic. I had actually jilted her graduation the summer before, because I was in a drunken stupor somewhere, and I didn't even bother to contact her afterwards. She only knew that I was going into the clinic when her dad showed her a newspaper cutting. While I was there I had no contact with the outside world, other than the letters that we wrote back and forth. This medieval form of communication had a profound effect on our relationship. There is an ability to be brutally honest when you write a letter; there is diminished shame and embarrassment at opening up your mind and heart to someone. In doing this, we forged a connection that is yet to be broken, and I pray that it never will, despite my continued failings.

When I left the clinic, I went back home and into an environment that wasn't conducive to sobriety. I was now living with all of the guys who I worked the London circuit with and, although they were incredibly supportive of what I was doing, they were still living the lives of young bachelors with a few quid in their pockets. I couldn't, and didn't, expect them to change just because I had a problem with booze. They were responsible drinkers and lived their lives as such, but it still offered me the temptation to join in on a daily basis. It challenged how much progress I had made with my 'people pleasing' mindset, and each time I refused an invitation to join them was a small victory in the war against it.

I couldn't be sure that I would always be this strong, though, and it really wasn't necessary to put myself in the middle of that temptation every day. As the weeks passed, I realised that without alcohol I had very little in common with my current circle of friends. Our relationships became strained, largely down to my own behaviours which really were shameful. I had been taking money out of the joint house bank account and replacing it at the end of the month. My drinking and gambling had put me into deep financial trouble. I had addressed the actions that had put me in this predicament, but I was still in the predicament itself.

It was so bad in my drinking days that at one point Ralf lent me his bank card to get some petrol for his car, but I took it to go on a bender for a couple of days, helping myself to cash out of his personal bank account. I still cringe to this day when I think back to some of those times when I was at my most desperate. It is part of the recovery programme to try to make amends to all those who you have wronged on your journey. I have repeatedly repented to all of my house-mates, some of whom accepted it and some of whom didn't. I'm fine about that – just because I apologise doesn't make everything better. I had to face the consequences of my actions, which in this case meant I lost several friendships that I will never get back.

I'd love to say that we all lived happily ever after from

here, but sadly that wasn't what happened; life with me just isn't that straightforward. I managed a couple of years of total sobriety, even getting through the promotion parties that followed the next summer when QPR were promoted to the Championship. I remember being on the coach back from Sheffield Wednesday, where we had clinched promotion on the final day of the season. There were two huge bins of beer and champagne in the aisle of the coach and the party was in full flow. I was equally as joyous but had to keep myself away from the ale. I was desperate to join in but very scared where it might take me. To indulge at the beginning of the summer break off the back of a successful season could have been a ticket straight back to Liphook, or maybe worse. Instead, I sat at the front of the bus next to the driver with a big Hoyo de Monterrey cigar and a four-pack of J2O, apple and melon if you are interested.

I carried on with this kind of resolve for many months, until I allowed myself to be persuaded that I had won the battle. I had a couple of glasses of wine when meeting friends one evening and happily went home at a reasonable hour, without the urge to make the night last forever. This was it, I told myself, I had beaten this terrible affliction. What I hadn't factored in was the capacity of my mind to do what is necessary. Of course I could do it, I had behaved like this previously and given up alcohol for long periods, so I knew it was within my capabilities.

I had never been the type of alcoholic who needs a bottle of vodka in the morning to function; I am not alcohol dependent. I am the type of alcoholic who loses conscious control when the poison takes hold. I repeatedly tried to put measures in place to ensure that this illusion of control seemed successful: I will only drink lager; I will only drink with Mrs C; I will go on only two big nights out per year, Christmas and the end of the season.

I managed to stick to these rules and, due to my ability to abstain for long periods of time, I assumed that I had it sussed. The reality was that I would only ever get in trouble twice a year. I don't just mean 'get told off by the missus' trouble, I mean something cataclysmic would happen whenever I had a big night out.

It came to one huge frothy head when I was on loan at Preston North End. We had a squad meal and night out in Manchester as a reward for completing a tough pre-season and to welcome the new season. Knowing that this was going to be a big one, we had rooms booked in the city centre and the gaffer had given us the next day off to recuperate. Determined to enjoy myself but show a level of responsibility, I did everything right that night. We ate, drank and made merry until the early hours. After a kip at the hotel and a decent breakfast, I made my way home back to Yorkshire. When I was pulled over by the police for 'routine checks' I was confident I'd be okay. I still felt a little hazy, as you do after a night out, but I wasn't worried. I should have been. I wasn't just over the limit – I was well over.

I was raging on the way back to the station, angry with myself: 'You are one royal fuck-up. I hope you're proud of yourself. You can't even get one night out right, can you?'

I wondered what on earth I was going to do. I felt sure that Gem would leave me and that I'd probably get sacked by Preston and/or Burnley. I thought I would definitely have to resign from the PFA. When will I learn that Clarke

Carlisle and alcohol just do not mix? When it's too late, that's when. I was charged and released later that day.

Ambling back to my car some ten miles away, I honestly believed that this was the end. I couldn't see any way that Gem would forgive me. I have returned home to interesting scenes before: my cases packed, my suits cut up and my collection of caps and trainers all dowsed in ink. I couldn't even begin to imagine what carnage would be waiting for me that day.

I called Gordon Taylor, the chief executive of the PFA, to tender my resignation. How could I represent the virtues of our members when I'd been done for drink driving? As you can imagine, he was bitterly disappointed when he heard what I had to say. To my surprise, though, he wouldn't accept my resignation. He wanted to try to help me through this time by getting to the root cause of the problem. He believed that that way there might be an opportunity for rehabilitation and redemption, as long as my remorse was sincere.

Sincere? I cannot convey how embarrassed, ashamed and utterly disgusted I was (and still am) about having this charge on my record. The circumstances of it are immaterial. Drink driving is one of those crimes where you have put the safety of everyone in jeopardy, whether you had an accident or not. The fact that I was stopped the next morning in no way diminishes the irresponsibility of my actions. I actually think it makes it worse. I was driving in the rush-hour traffic, in school-run traffic, in situations where an error of judgement would more likely cause huge collateral damage. I am thankful that I wasn't involved in an accident and that I can contribute to helping others become aware of the dangers of 'the morning after the night before'.

— CHAPTER 15 —

HALF THE WORLD AWAY

After I'd been done for drink driving, I went to court and was banned from driving for 20 months, and given a £4000 fine. And this is why I am currently using trains, buses and taxis to get everywhere. Mrs C did pretty much kick me out. I rented a flat on the docks in Preston in order to be able to get to training and matches with relative ease. It was during this time away from my family, alone with my own thoughts, that I really started to consciously struggle with my mind. I had been reading about the symptoms of depression, and they all seemed incredibly familiar.

This was because of the discussions that Gem and I had been having after I had failed to support her when she was suffering from post-natal depression; I didn't understand it. I couldn't grasp how she could be depressed when our life seemed so good, with a lifestyle that those we had grown up with could barely have dreamed of. I wondered why she didn't just get a grip and see how good life was. But when I looked into it more, I realised that depression is an illness and indiscriminate, which encouraged me to learn more about the condition.

The more I learnt, the louder the alarm bells rang. So, in the quiet of my own room, I took the Goldberg test online, slightly intrigued as to whether I might be starting to drop into depression. The results on the screen must have been wrong, so I reloaded it and did it again, adjusting a couple of my answers for ones that I thought would probably represent a healthier mind. The results popped up on the screen a second time.

'You are suffering with severe depression. Please consult your GP immediately.'

Shit.

My first response was that I couldn't be depressed: I am a professional footballer, and I have used the techniques taught to me by some of the best psychologists in the game to be able to perform under extreme pressure. This must be wrong.

I decided to call the club doctor at Preston to ask him about it. Again, I was able to place myself in the trust of a brilliant human being. The doc ran through the test with me again and confirmed that the outcome was correct. It was now that I actually started to treat my depression medically for the first time in my life. This wasn't as mind-blowing a revelation as it once might have been. I understood a lot more about the nature of depression after reading up on post-natal depression with Mrs C. Finding out what the illness actually is and how it manifests itself is a process that liberates you from the stigma about the 'D' word.

The truth is that being diagnosed with 'something' was a very significant moment for me. There have been so many times I've berated myself and been completely self-deprecating because of the way that I have been thinking or feeling that to have a logical and clinical reason for it gave me a sense of hope. I must clarify that learning I had depression wasn't an excuse on which to blame all of my past actions and behaviours. I still take complete responsibility for the decisions that I have made in my life, but it served as an explanation for why my thought processes were so illogical and why many of my decisions were so ill-judged.

Taking my daily dose of fluoxetine has made an unbelievable difference to my life. Knowing that they're not 'happy pills' (although that is how I refer to them in jest) is something I had to educate myself about in order to be comfortable taking them. The pills don't make me happy, they adjust the chemical levels in my brain so that I can view life from a balanced perspective. Another point to make is that they don't make things perfect – life is still a bitch! But the bonus is that I can face all of my issues and problems with a clear head and an element of objectivity, and that is a huge difference. In fact, treating my depression can make the difference between drink or no drink, bet or no bet, life or death. Dramatic, I know, but the evidence is there for you to see.

The outcome of all of this is that I have been to some very interesting places and witnessed some bizarre things, all under the influence of the green fairy and her many friends. I would be a bare-faced liar if I told you that I hated every minute of it. I had some phenomenal times on nights out and have several tales that I'd love to share. The lawyers have told me I can't, so you'll have to settle for these instead! The bravado and machismo of lads on a night out is the same the nation over. Add to that a little bit of fame or infamy, a bit more money in the pocket and a lifestyle that certain women seem to aspire to get on board with, then the antics can lead to some ridiculous outcomes. They range from hilarious to stupid to downright wrong and I'll let you categorise them according to your own moral compass.

The first tale of note was on a Christmas do with Burnley. We were on our way down to Cardiff for a Championship fixture in early December and had made our plans to stay over afterwards and spend two nights in the Welsh capital. We were travelling down on the team bus the day before, and the snow was falling with intent. Just as we passed junction 16 of the M6 the manager, Brian Laws, received the phone call that we had all been hoping for: the game was off. Anyone would have thought we'd won the league. The two-day party had just become a three-day event and there was no hiding everyone's excitement at the prospect. The coach pulled over on the A500 as we held an emergency meeting at the back. We didn't want to carry on to Cardiff, as the roads were murder and that would cost us several hours of good drinking time. After a couple of phone calls and a round or two of voting, it was decided. We would take the bus to Nottingham and spend the weekend there. We could be in the pub in less than two hours and begin the mother of all Christmas parties. But there was just one problem: the manager and his staff were still with us on the bus.

'What do you expect us to do?' asked the gaffer.

'Don't worry, we can call you a cab from here; Beasty knows a local cab company.'

'You can't just drop us off at the side of the motorway!' the boss protested.

After a couple of quick conversations, we decided that it wouldn't be right to dump them at the side of the road.

'Okay, gaffer. We'll take you back to the last services and you can get a cab from there.'

I don't think that any other manager I've worked under would have allowed that to happen, but there was far more power in the dressing room than in Brian Laws's hands. So we commandeered the coach and wended our merry way over to Nottingham.

After a night drinking copious amounts of alcohol at a ridiculous pace, we ended up back at the hotel where a couple of lads and I began to wrestle in the corridor. For some unknown reason, we thought it would be a good idea to do this naked. We endured a couple of rounds of WWE before the night guard came up to warn us about the noise. He was a nice guy, very reasonable, and had some kind of injury to his leg. He limped up the corridor and tried to hush the group. At this point in the evening, there was no reason in the minds of the lads and the guard was sent packing down to reception amid drunken comments and slurred attempts at banter. When he returned ten minutes later he was far more assertive.

'You have to calm down and go to your rooms or I will call the police,' he said.

'You had better go back downstairs before we set the dog on you,' replied one of the boys.

'Pardon?'

'We'll let the dog out if you're not careful.'

'Don't be ridiculous. You don't have a dog, now get to your rooms.'

'Okay, we warned you. Let him out!'

At which point the door to one of the rooms was flung open and I bounded out on all fours barking like a bull mastiff. The guard's face turned from incredulity to dismay to terror in a few short instants. I was tearing down the corridor like a greyhound at Walthamstow, eyes fixed on this confused and debilitated man. He turned around and started to make a run for the lift, well, more a hobble as his leg was seriously impeding his progress. He kept glancing over his shoulder, desperately trying to make the call button as I got closer and closer. About ten yards away I could see the whites of his eyes as he shouted: 'Why are you naked?!'

Then I pounced, nibbled the guy on the inside of his leg like he was my local postman and I was the neighbourhood hound. He was frantically pushing the lift button and collapsed through the doors as soon as it arrived, while I trotted back to complete round five of the naked Royal Rumble.

Needless to say, I had to apologise profusely for this event and I still don't know how we got there. The hound is not my usual party trick; it's usually the three-second pint or the Carlisle Shuffle (the worst dance move you've ever seen), but the Junkyard Dog is a memory that will not be forgotten.

This wasn't the only time that Brian didn't react exactly how I would expect my gaffer to. We were in Portugal later that season, staying in some beautiful villas in Vale do Lobo for a bit of a break away from the normal daily grind. It was a time to relax and enjoy ourselves, and the trip's shenanigans had already resulted in the boss's table-tennis table being deposited in the swimming pool, along with all of his outside furniture, set up as though it was a sub-aqua retreat. After a second night on the ale, Chris Eagles and I awoke to find that the bus had already left for a light training session. We ordered a cab to take us down to the pitch and clambered inside. As we were about to set off, the gaffer jumped into the front seat alongside the driver as he had missed the bus, too. This would have been fine, apart from the fact that I was sitting there in just my pants and a pair of tan brogues, nothing else, discussing with Chris whether I should keep my Sloggis on or train in just the shoes. Noticing the gaffer in the front, I asked him what he thought.

'I'm just glad you've turned up,' was his response, much to our delight. When we arrived at the training pitch, I clambered out of the cab and proceeded to warm up Eastern European style, star jumps et al, much to the hilarity of my colleagues – Sloggis on, fyi!

The excitement that envelops a squad before a Christmas do is only matched by the anxiety of our partners. Every year it's the same. The weeks leading up to the party are littered with squabbles, arguments and threats about what will happen if you get into trouble. I've known some players who have completely manufactured an argument, just to ensure that there is a viable reason to be in a mood when the party is in full flow. It's completely understandable as well, because there will be someone who gets into some kind of trouble at some point; whether it's with girls, guys or the police, something will happen.

One common ploy to escape the wrath of the missus is to 'lose' your phone or have it 'stolen'. The amount of phones that have disappeared on the way to a Christmas do or that are stolen over the weekend is matched only by the number of phones that actually do get lost or thrown in a pint pot over the weekend. There was one lad whose wife had been calling incessantly throughout the night without any success in getting through to him. Her worst fears seemed to have been realised when someone finally picked up the phone at 7.30am, and it was a woman's voice she heard.

'Who the hell is this and where is my husband?!'

'Don't panic, love,' replied the voice. 'I've just found this phone, I'm a cleaner.'

A wave of relief washed over her: 'Oh, right. Can you keep it there and I'll get him to come and pick it up?'

'Sure, I'll just leave it on reception here.'

'Excellent, thanks. Where do you work?'

'Spearmint Rhino.'

This is the second certainty of the do, some (if not all) of the lads will end up at a strip club at some point in the weekend. It is usually on the Sunday afternoon, if there isn't a decent match to watch on the big screen, but some will go each night as a natural climax to the evening, usually as another group (the one that I tend to be in) makes its way to the casino.

I am not going to get all self-righteous about strip joints; I've been to more than a fair few in my time, but they're just not my preferred option. I don't see the point in paying money to watch someone get their boobs out, especially when there are plenty of boobs on show for free at most nightclubs nowadays. Secondly, I much prefer the thrill of the chase. Actually engaging with females and winning them over is far more enjoyable and rewarding, even when there is no intention to take it any further. It is a huge massage of the ego to know that you've still got it, even if there is no intention to seal the deal. The trouble is that my ability to draw that line is severely impaired when copious amounts of alcohol are involved. The third reason for not wanting to go is that I would much rather be at the casino. I had little hesitation in being the only person to make the break for the tables and would happily sit there for hours getting lost in the machines and roulette. 'Five, red, odd' is still a phrase that gives me a little rush, but chasing that rush is the reason why I'm in my current financial position.

The casino has an ability to draw me in because I find total escapism in there. It is another sure-fire symptom of depression, the need to get away from the mental state that I'm currently in. I get lost in the maths of it all, in the odds, in the permutations of bets and, ultimately, that ephemeral buzz that you get when you beat all the odds of the house. It is a fleeting and incredibly dangerous way to try to reproduce the enormous emotional high that football creates; fleeting because the longer you stay, the more the house will ultimately take off you, dangerous because you end up chasing your money as well as your fleeting high.

I remember falling out of Tokyo Joe's in Preston one time and heading down to Refreshment Village, the kebab shop of choice at the time. On my strangely circuitous route there, I literally stumbled across a homeless guy who asked for some change.

'When did you last sleep in a bed?' I asked.

'I don't know,' said the guy.

'Right, come with me,' I ordered, as I hailed a passing cab. I could see that the fellow was extremely hesitant to listen to this inebriated kid on the street, and he warily approached the door of the cab.

'What do you want from me?' he asked.

'Nothing, fella. We're gonna get you a shower and a bed.'

'Why?'

'Because it's bloody Baltic out here and you need one,'

which he did, his odour was overpowering even to a drunkard. He got in the cab and pressed himself as far into the opposite corner from me as possible. We drove around four different hotels until we got to The Tickled Trout. The night porter told me the place was full, but I pleaded and appealed to his good nature.

'Look, mate. I just want this guy to have a shower and a bed. If you make that happen then there's a little something in it for you too.'

He paused a while and then eventually let us in. He gave me the key to a room which I paid for, with a little bit more besides, and I passed it on to my new friend. He took it from me and just stood there, looking at me, waiting.

'Go on then,' I said.

'What? Are we . . . ?'

'No danger! I'm going home. Go and get a good night's sleep.' And off I went.

The guy was understandably nervous, especially because I was drunk, but it still makes me laugh that he was dead sure I was grooming him. Can't a kid do something without an ulterior motive any more?

Money is often a guarantee to get you where you want to go on a night out. The ridiculous sums spent by a group of footballers and the kudos for an establishment at their presence will usually outweigh the trouble or mess that duly follows. I have often used money to try to get into places or around dress codes. I remember being outside Chinawhites in central London one time and the bouncer was adamant that the club was full and no one else was coming in. I sidled to the front of the queue with my mate in tow and beckoned the burly doorman over. As he approached I pulled a £50 note out of my wallet, slowly folded it up and placed it in the breast pocket of his suit with a little tap.

'Thank you very much,' he said. 'But the club is still full, no one's coming in and, when they do, you'll have to get to the back of the queue because you've lost your place.'

I sloped off with my tail between my legs and cursing the guy under my breath like Dick Dastardly.

Pre-season trips were also bankers for a good night out. The entire squad is present, so there can't be any excuses about permission from partners or troubles with babysitters; the 'disco pass' is a complete freebie and it is treasured. My first experience of this was at QPR when we went down to Torquay, or somewhere similarly glamorous, in the summer of 2000. We were allowed one night out and the lads made the most of it.

The best trips I had were definitely with Burnley under Owen Coyle – USA, Scotland, Malaysia and Ireland – we affectionately referred to them as 'Stag Do 08', 'Stag Do 09' and so on. Though Owen himself is teetotal, it was mandatory to meet in the Irish bar every night of the trip. I must stress that drinking wasn't compulsory, but when you had a squad that included Steve Caldwell, Michael Duff, Stevie Jordan, Graham Alexander, Robbie Blake and myself, it was inevitable. That group was the most hardened bunch of drinkers that I have ever come across in my life, whether in or out of football. Some of the sessions that we went on were epic. Even when the 'next generation' came on board, the likes of David Edgar, Danny Fox and Kevin McDonald, the level of consumption didn't drop, it was just the poison of choice that changed.

Imagine our surprise, then, when a new signing joined

us on a night out for the first time and declared: 'I will definitely be the last man standing. I will see all you ladies in the morning.'

We didn't say anything, but one or two eyebrows were raised. We set off on the night out around Singapore and the drinking pace was supersonic and relentless, owing not least in part to my voracious thirst. We were all herded into a cordoned-off area at a club that had been prearranged by our tour hosts, and the drinks kept coming like a Yo Sushi conveyor belt. A couple of hours in, I could see the lads huddled around a chair at the front of the section, all taking photos and laughing their heads off, so I wandered down to see what was going on. There was Chris Iwelumo, Mr Last Man Standing, slumped over with his head between his legs and two full bottles of beer in his hands. It was beautiful. He was packed off before midnight and apologised unreservedly in the morning for his poor showing. Needless to say, he never made such a bold statement again.

But, as I said earlier, I am trying to put all this sort of behaviour behind me. I distanced myself from the planned festivities for this year and started to get my head around the change in my circumstances. However, even if I wasn't going to be drinking, I knew that one of the imminent unavoidable events was one that I have seen destroy many a player before: the new boy karaoke. Every club that I've been at has had the tradition of getting the new signing to sing for the lads after dinner at their first overnight trip. From QPR back in 2000 to York City this season, I have always belted out Bob Marley's 'Three Little Birds' and I am extremely confident in my rendition.

With this being my second spell at Northampton, a repeat

performance wasn't acceptable, so I needed a new song. I spent days listening to music and practising something that would suit my dulcet tones, but nothing would fit. I didn't want to go the way of many I've witnessed before. Lads have been struck mute, come out in full sweats, completely forgotten the lyrics to simple songs like 'Wonderwall' and even fallen off the chair that is their mock stage. It is so strange that a player can easily walk out on a pitch in front of tens of thousands of people and play football, but get him in a dining room in front of his 20 team-mates and he is a quivering wreck. The reality is that it is not his comfort zone. Football is what we do, it's what we train to do and it is what we're relatively confident about doing. Singing is not.

One of the funniest examples of this that I saw was Chris Eagles. When he arrived at Watford on loan he was but a young pup. He stood up on the chair ready to belt out a tune and then just seemed to lose all co-ordination. He cherried up in the face and started to wobble all over the place. All of a sudden, he completely collapsed, sweat pouring from his forehead, and then hurried out of the restaurant not to be seen again until the following morning. This scarred him so much that when he arrived at Burnley he was adamant that he would not be singing. It took us six months to grind him down, and even then he didn't actually sing. He ended up just telling us an incredibly funny story about some random people turning up in his hotel room one night. Some guy was brought in by the hotel staff, and Chrissy assumed he was a director or something, sharing a room for the night. While he was sat on his bed in his pants, this guy started to unpack and was making polite conversation. It was only when he asked Chris which company he worked for and how many conventions he'd been to that they both realised there had been a huge mistake. Chrissy was just relieved that he had had his back, sack and crack done and was in a presentable state.

There has only ever been one person that I can remember who has flatly refused to sing or pay the corresponding fine for that, and that was Tyrone Mears. He is an incredibly shy lad at the best of times and this was territory that he was just not going to be made to occupy.

Finally I found a song that would work for me, and I approached it like I do most things in my life: giving it everything I've got. I belted out an ear-splitting rendition of 'Half The World Away' by Oasis and the lads were very impressed, not with the quality of my voice – cats have died more melodiously – but with the conviction I gave it. I returned to my seat at the dinner table and could finally relax and enjoy my meal. In truth, sitting there without a drink in my hand, I felt half a world away from some of the places I've been.

— CHAPTER 16 —

WINTER BLUES AND GREEN FINGERS

I'm nearly halfway through this season and I haven't discussed much about what I do in my spare time. There's quite a simple reason for this: I don't even know what spare time is. I have a window between 6.15 and 6.20 on Thursdays when I can fart. It's the run-up to Christmas, I've just changed clubs, football has its ethical tremors, I have three assignments due before semester end and half a dozen meetings with different charities to squeeze in. What's the last thing I would have time to do now? Move house!

I collapsed on the sofa when I returned home after training and Mrs C dropped a mini bombshell. She wants to be near her family in North Yorkshire because we are quite isolated here, on the edge of Saddleworth Moor. Because I'm spending so much time away, Gem hasn't got a network of people around her. We chose our current house because it is equidistant between both of our families, roughly an hour and a half each way. It seemed a good decision at the time but, in hindsight, has turned out to be a big mistake. We are neither here nor there. It is a conscious effort for any family member to visit, no one can just 'pop over' like Gem was used to in her upbringing, and how she would like our family home to be. Being in either Yorkshire or Lancashire would have allowed that open-door relationship to develop, but being on the periphery has resulted in long periods of loneliness for us, and more severely for Gem.

I dropped a text to a neighbour who expressed an interest in buying our house earlier in the year, thinking he would tell us where to go seeing as we knocked him back. To my surprise he jumped at the offer and asked if we could be out next week. Right, it's on. We need to find a house, school and a shitload of money in the next few weeks – absolutely no pressure or stress there at all. Meanwhile, I've got to head back down to Northampton tomorrow, starting with a 5.30 taxi, and I have £20 to feed myself for the next three days. How the hell has it come to this?

It's funny, we walked into the Trafford Centre last week for the first time in months (oh, how we miss that place) and I said to Gem: 'Do you remember when we used to be here every week, shopping with reckless abandon? How times change, and how I wish I wasn't a feckless waster of money!'

It is generally the same at most clubs that I've been at: Wednesdays and Sundays are your days off, giving you a chance to relax with the family, enjoy your other hobbies or just kick back and relax. At the moment for me, each Wednesday comes and goes but there is no relaxation in sight. Instead of getting back to be with my family, last week I set off on the train from Northampton to Loughborough for a UKAD athletes committee meeting. This is a committee that is formed of athletes from many of the different sporting disciplines, and we met to discuss the implications of and issues surrounding anti-doping rules across UK sport.

It was only an hour away, but that meant three trains, and I was still lugging my big team bag around with me. It's seen some mileage for a bag that's never left the country. What's bonkers is that I don't have a single penny to my name. I booked the Loughborough train online with Mrs C's card, but I have zero access to cash. Not only did I cadge two lifts, but I had to duck and dive to take the direct route back to Yorkshire, instead of the Northampton route that I came by. It was lucky that no one checked my ticket the whole way. It saved me three hours of travel time, so that I could spend a little more time with my family.

This week I have to go to university. I am studying for a BA in Professional Sports Writing and Broadcasting at Staffordshire University. It is a course tailor-made by the university and the PFA so that current professionals can still study while playing. It's 5.22 in the morning and I had a tough match last night. The last time I looked at my clock it was 3.38 and I still hadn't managed to disperse the adrenaline and get any sleep. My eyes are burning; I feel sick and am seriously wondering if this is worth it. ITV have already started discussions on a possible contract to work with them, so why am I doing this? I suppose it's another one of those situations where I have to prove myself. And of course I can't just 'get a degree'; I am allegedly intelligent, so nothing less than a first will do. There is also the fact that I've started it and I've told people about it, so I can't quit now. The voice in my head is being so paranoid: 'People will say you failed, that you can't do it, that you're faux intelligent and it's all a charade. You must get on that train . . .'

I know I have to do it. I don't want to be the standard 'ex-footballer pundit' who thinks that he can stroll into a job on the telly just because he managed to play the game for a while. I really feel that gaining an education in the industry will add a little bit of kudos to any ideas or opinions that I have when I try to make the crossover. I wearily make my way to uni and get through the day, knowing that it will all be worth it in the long run. It is a tad different to most students' university experience, though. While I'm there, I end up having to participate in interviews with the other students for their own work. There just isn't a day when I can switch off from football.

This could be the most exciting day I've had all year. I have had my application through to get my driving licence back. Being without a car is one of the most inconvenient things in the world. It is a deserved punishment for what I did, and I can categorically state that I will not make the same mistake again. The implications aren't just about travel and having to use public transport, it's the expense, too.

Many of the meetings that I have to attend are called at very short notice. Getting a train to London without an advance booking is as expensive as flying to the South of France – it's ludicrous. Then you're beholden to the train schedules, transport links and inevitable delays. Home life is just as difficult. There's no 'popping to the shops', especially with two kids in tow. Doing the school run is a military mission and costs £20 in taxi fares. Getting over to see my daughter Francesca is just nigh-on impossible: three hours on trains, grab a couple of hours together and three hours back in order to be at training the next day.

Getting my licence back will make such a huge difference to my daily life, but getting a car is another challenge again. I'm genuinely not sure if we can afford to run two cars. It's not just the outlay on the actual vehicle; insurance costs for a footballer are extortionate. With a clean licence my premium was over £3000; I dread to think what it will cost with a drink-driving endorsement. The answer is simple: too much. Most insurers won't even look at me and those who will are quoting figures around the £7000 mark. I'm going to need some help in order to get back on the road, but it's something that I need to do.

There are certain times when I just have to slap myself in the face and put my life into perspective. I've had a manic day off again today. Buses, taxis and trains have been the order of the day as I travelled over to Merseyside to do some filming. By the time I arrived, I was feeling extremely sorry for myself, cursing the fact that I don't have this and I still need to do that and it would all be so much better if I just had the other. Then I started to focus on the reason why I was there and I felt like a spoilt little brat.

I am proud to be one of the patrons of the Katy Holmes Trust. Katy first entered my world when she was a mascot for Preston North End last season. She was full of smiles and excitement and reminded me a lot of Francesca. Just two months afterwards, we were informed that she had been diagnosed with a brain tumour and was spending time in a local hospice, Derian House. I went over with a few of the squad to visit Katy in there and two things really struck me. Firstly, I couldn't believe how amazing this young girl was, still smiling and happy even though this terrible disease had gripped her life and was radically transforming her body. Secondly, the warmth, strength and unity of her family were something to behold. Her parents, Paula and David, showed me exactly what love is.

When we left, I could not get the family out of my mind. I felt so guilty because I often take my health and that of my family for granted. I genuinely do not know what I would do if I had to deal with that situation. My love for my children is the most powerful emotion in my world; I couldn't even begin to imagine what they were enduring as a family. What I could do, though, was offer my support in any way possible that could help their cause. They were attempting to raise funds to get Katy overseas for special treatment that isn't available on these shores.

They were well on the way to reaching that target when, on 19 January 2012, she passed away. I had just started to get involved with what the family were doing and the news hit me hard. I called Gem in tears at what had happened and with feelings of utter despair for the family. If I felt like this, I wondered how on earth they must be feeling. Well, Paula came hurtling out of her grieving process with a passion and determination that I have never witnessed before. She is doing everything she can to raise awareness about paediatric brain tumours and change the way that cancer research funding is distributed. This lady will not be stopped.

When she asked if I would be a patron for the trust, I cried again and was honoured that she asked me. I am incredibly proud to be associated with what KHT are doing; I just wish I could do more. Today, I was helping to film an internet trailer for the trust. It was a solo piece where I talk through my experience with Katy and her family. It never fails to move me to tears, and it always refills my appreciation levels for what I have in my life. If you do one thing this year, please just click on their website and lend your support, they're changing lives.

Something else that I have had to sort out because of my imminent return to the road is my eyesight. I had an eye test a couple of years ago and they told me that I need glasses for driving, but then I got banned, so in one way at least my ban saved me a fortune. So before I got my licence back, I needed to get my eyes reassessed and get myself goggled up. I went to an optician in Northampton and they told me that I need to wear glasses for 'any periods of concentration'. Surely that means all the time, then? I thought they were just trying to siphon a bit more money out of my pocket, until I put the glasses on. Wow, it was like life, but in HD! I could not believe the difference that glasses made to my general eyesight. I had been noticing in recent months that my facial recognition at around half a pitch was terrible. I could see that there was someone there but I couldn't tell you who it was unless they were blatantly distinguishable, like Bayo. Now all of a sudden I could read signs at 200 paces again – it was glorious.

I asked whether I should wear contact lenses for matches, but they didn't think it would be necessary. The glasses would take the strain off my eyes in general daily life, so when it came to focusing without additional help for 90 minutes, they should be fine. And they were absolutely right. I found that my vision improved almost immediately and it really made a difference to my performance. The only drawback was the inevitable stick that I got for arriving to work with my new glasses on. It was all light-hearted banter and the biggest compliment I got was that some people thought I wore glasses anyway, so they didn't even notice anything different. The first time I wore them on the box was a different matter, though. I got a barrage of stick on Twitter, including the predictable: 'What a twat, just trying to look clever.'

To which I replied: 'No, just trying to look.'

It was fairly witty, but also it was true. Why do people have to be so judgemental? It can be really tiresome at times. What is extremely unhelpful at a moment of insecurity like this is when your nearest and dearest pulls no punches. I sent Gem a picture of me in my new glasses and asked what she thought. 'Have you considered laser surgery?' she asked. Thanks, love, for that vote of confidence.

I'm not going to pretend I don't care what Gem thinks, either. If I'm honest, she has moulded me from the day we met. I used to be a Reebok Classic, Fred Perry t-shirt-wearing drum and bass enthusiast when we first got to know each other. Now I wear either basketball gear or suits, have a body covered in tattoos and never leave the toilet seat up. My music choice hasn't changed; she won't get me away from my love of LTJ Bukem. My music taste has progressed actually, and is now even more to Mrs C's disliking. I have started to listen to a lot of classical music, especially on long drives. Smooth classics at two on Classic FM is incredibly relaxing. It's probably quite rare to get someone who is enthusiastic about these totally different genres, but I think they both offer the same thing: an opportunity to let a piece of music grab you and take you to another place, to get lost in the intensity or the flow and let your mind improvise its own script to the musical journey. Not when Gem's in the car, though; it's Jay-Z, Jill Scott or nothing.

Winter is upon us. I bloody hate this time of year. I have self-diagnosed a case of Raynaud's disease, but, whether it is actually this or not, I have a considerable problem with the circulation of blood in my fingers and toes. It doesn't even need to be cold. The weather at training today was probably best described as 'mild', yet my fingers still went luminous yellow due to the hyper-constriction of my blood vessels.

It has been a problem for my whole life. I remember crying as a young boy playing Sunday football because of the pain that this causes. Why does it have to hurt so much? Not only do you suffer the inconvenience of having no feeling in your phalanges, but it gets so bad that they sometimes lock like some kind of fake claw. The worst part of it all is when the blood starts to flow through them again. After training today, I regressed to that nine-year-old boy again. I was huddled in the corner of the showers, curled up in an almost foetal position, grunting and shouting, trying to hold back the tears that were desperate to flow from my eyes. The pain is horrific. It starts as pins and needles, then progresses to a throb that syncs with your pulse, and culminates in a constant, searing pain that feels like your hands are about to explode. My hands become a mini-rainbow as each finger changes from yellow to green to purple to bright red, and not in unison. One finger sometimes stays green throughout it all and ends up glowing next to the others which have completed the cycle. Cowering in the corner, I'm overwhelmed by the concern of my team-mates.

'What are you doing, you freak?'

'Look at my fingers.'

'Ugh, you freak. What the hell is that?'

Thanks, lads. It doesn't always feel this bad – probably

only once a week – but any day the temperature is in single figures or below, the magic fingers will appear.

The weather has a huge impact on our training sessions, too. When the ground freezes there is no way that we can train on the pitches. They're a safety hazard for starters. Knees and ankles are always the first to go because it's like playing on concrete, the only difference being that pitches never freeze as a truly flat surface, especially not at Sixfields. Because of this, we have to find somewhere else to train, and this is usually at the local Goals five-a-side centre. The artificial surface here means we can at least do some kind of training. Some of the squad can't take part at all if they have prior ankle, knee or back problems that may be aggravated by the firmness of the pitches, so it really disrupts any kind of team play or tactical training that the gaffer may want to do. We can get a sweat on, though, and we'd much rather do that by playing football than having to run our nuts off at the track.

The training ground being out of bounds can often result in some improvised sessions. Aidy took us to our local cage-fighting club and made us train with the instructors there. We walked through the door and the first guy we saw had the physique of Buster Bloodvessel, with tattoos down his face and a vest that he could only possibly have purchased at Gap Kids, it was that tight. I'm not saying that we were at all intimidated, but even Bayo was quiet. I don't know if it was just the instructor's style, but he didn't seem to be very happy that this bunch of namby-pamby footballers was in his gym. He set about a session that seemed more like a demonstration of how soft we were and how fearless he was.

That being said, the workout was very enjoyable, apart

from one incident. I was squared up with Bayo, 19 stones of brawn snarling at me like I was his main course. The idea was to tap the other person's ankle while making sure that they didn't tap yours. It sounds easy, sounds friendly, sounds safe. Not when you get two ultra-competitive men opposite one another, both over six feet tall and both with huge heads. We jockeyed around for all of a minute, feinting, taunting, psyching each other out, then, as if we were on a timer, we both made a diving lunge for the other's ankle. The echo from our heads colliding rang around the whole gym. I would usually fancy my chances in a clash of heads against anyone, but this was one strong head. B had also gone in with his head down, whereas I was still trying to keep my eye on the target. This meant that the top of his head met flush with the bridge of my nose. We hit the floor and rolled away from each other. I was seeing stars as I clambered to my feet and I already had the metallic taste in my mouth, the unmistakable flavour of blood from my damaged nose. B, on the other hand, seemed oblivious to the contact.

'I got you fam, yeah. That's what you get when you test me.'

This guy is merciless. If this is how he treats his friends I don't ever want to get on his bad side.

This isn't the first time I've finished training with a blood-ied nose. Back at QPR in 2000, I remember us training on the lawn in front of our hotel, the morning of a match. It was genuine 'jumpers for goalposts' stuff. I thought we'd just have a nice easy session to get ready for the game, so I got a shock when Iain Dowie accidentally caught me with a forearm smash in the face. I wouldn't have minded if it hadn't been for the fact that he was our coach.

There have been plenty of other utterly random training sessions. Earlier this season with York, we made the long journey down to Southend. When we got there we were stiff and tired, looking forward to a good night's kip.

'Right, half an hour to get changed and we'll meet you outside.'

These were not the words I wanted to hear. It was cold, wet and getting late. We reconvened in the lobby and took a walk down to the beach, a bag of balls in tow. Surely we weren't going to try to play football on the beach, not in this weather? No, we weren't. We proceeded to play playground games of over under, tunnel ball and kicking a ball up the sea wall! It was clearly made up as they went along, but it was actually really fun and a good way to get the journey out of the legs.

These unusual sessions can be quite nice from time to time; they break up the monotony of what is usually a highly regimented schedule. They're not so great when you have to improvise training every single day. This could be one of the consistently coldest winters that I have ever experienced. There is absolutely no letting up with this weather. We have had a period of two weeks so far where we haven't been able to train on grass once, and even the artificial surface is too dangerous do anything on. Sessions are being improvised on a daily basis and it all seems a bit ridiculous.

We are getting to a match on a Saturday having not kicked a ball for the entire week, which just can't be right. The worst moment of it all is when your match on a Saturday is called off, too. It may be something that we do regularly, but it is still the emotional and psychological focus of the week. Everything that we do is geared towards the game. You prepare yourself by whatever routine you have to make sure that you are ready to perform at three o'clock on a Saturday afternoon, so when that is taken away from you, it all feels like a huge anticlimax.

It is a two-pronged problem. Firstly, the crescendo of your week needs to be replaced; the high of performing needs to be achieved in some way or another. This used to be with a night out, but I can find as much satisfaction in spending a full day with my family now; I am definitely getting old. Secondly, this match will have to be rearranged for another time, probably a Tuesday night, meaning that we will have a pile-up of fixtures when it comes to the business end of the season. The fewer postponed games we have, the better; there are only so many Saturday-Tuesday-Saturday weeks that my body can handle any more.

I have got my car back – woo hoo! One of the perks of being a footballer is that the PFA have business partnerships with many firms who subsequently offer special discounted rates to the members. We have been able to get two cars for the same monthly payment that we were outlaying for just Gem's car previously, an absolute bargain. The only draw-back is that we have to give a deposit of £2000 per car, and also need to pay £2500 to hand Gem's old car back. If it wasn't for the money I've just received for writing this book, there's no way I could have afforded it, but I need to get on the road. I am going to have to be a media whore for a little while to pay for them, but they'll be worth it – and not least because mine is a Mercedes C63 AMG. It has a 6.3 litre engine, which is utterly ludicrous and incredibly thirsty, but fortunately Northampton are paying for my petrol to get to work and back, so that is a rather sizeable cost that I am spared. It also means that I must get on and finish the book.

I had one of the more unusual experiences in my career during today's game. I went up for the first corner of the match and the guy marking me asked: 'Is that Creed?'

He was talking about my aftershave, and indeed it was.

'I'll be sticking close to you, then,' he said with a grin.

A little later in the game, we were tussling in the box, jostling for position before the ball came in, when the referee blew his whistle and called us both over. 'Put a stop to the games, fellas,' he said.

'Have you smelt him? He smells bloody lovely,' said my marker, putting a smile on all of our faces.

— CHAPTER 17 —

THE CHRISTMAS ONESIE

The dream life continues back in the Northampton Travelodge. The room smells and there are little burn holes in the curtains, this is awesome. I am so done with this. The travelling is killing me and the emotional rewards don't seem to be there any more. We win a game, great; we lose a game, great; we draw a game, great. As long as I have performed well, I don't seem to be overly concerned about the result, which isn't like me at all. However, my main preoccupation is that I just need to make sure I'm playing the next week because we need the income. I never thought that football would get to this stage for me. It feels like I need football but football doesn't need me. What a horrible thought.

I'm sitting here in the lead-up to Christmas and I haven't bought any presents, I'm not feeling at all 'Christmassy', we're about to move out of our house so have got even less money and, even if I had some, I haven't got time to fart at the moment. I'd love to go AWOL. I'd love to join the party season and fill my boots. But therein lies the reason that I can't, because I probably would go AWOL. What a sobering

190

thought. I suppose this is progress, knowing the circumstances in which I would be likely to fall back into my old ways. But being aware of these feelings and actually stopping them are two different things. However, I've stopped them today, and that's all I can do. For that reason I'm still married, still got my family, can still go to work tomorrow and I'm still chairman at the union. If I ever need any reminders to keep me on the straight and narrow, then Gem and the kids are as long as the list needs to be.

I'm beginning to feel a little more like Alan Partridge as each day goes by. The petrol station by the hotel has a Marks and Spencer in it, so today I'm plumping for some salmon and a superbean salad. I know I'd rather walk across the road and get a fat burger from TGI Fridays, but there has to be a sliver of self-discipline.

Christmas is a funny time of year. When the world and its dog are getting ready for an extended holiday period that is filled with gluttony and excess, footballers are preparing for one of the busiest sections of our season. I have had only one Christmas day off in the last 16 years. Every year we have to come in and train, preparing for the Boxing Day fixture. It isn't too bad when it is a home game, because you can generally return home and at least sample the Christmas fayre. When it is an away game, however, the only delights you get to enjoy are an under-staffed hotel, with under-motivated employees who shut up every facility as early as possible. You can't get so much as a piece of toast on Christmas Day night, while your family are in a food and alcohol-induced coma in some other part of the country. I hope they develop gout. I'm only kidding.

This is the norm for us, and I just get on with it. Mrs C,

on the other hand, is absolutely desperate for us to have a 'normal' Christmas. At the beginning of the season we thought that this might be the year. York had a home fixture so, even if we had to train on Christmas Day, I would have been able to eat dinner at home and spend the evening with the family. Delighted at the prospect, Gem invited all of the family around to our house and she had big plans for the day. However, transferring to Northampton meant that my game wouldn't be in York on Boxing Day, but in bloody Wimbledon. Not only would I not spend Christmas Day or night with my family, I wouldn't even be there on Christmas Eve. Sod's bloody law.

I attempted to placate her by saying that this could be the last year that we have to do this at Christmas, but my words fell on deaf ears. I can cope with Gem being upset about it, as she understands the reasons, even if she doesn't like them, but when my son Marley cried about it I realised that the goalposts had moved somewhat. Children can't understand the reasons for certain things. I tried to explain to him that 'Daddy has to work; I have to get money so that we can pay bills and buy things', but he asked why I didn't just get some money from the bank.

Marley hates football. He sees it as the reason that Daddy is away all the time and why Daddy has cuts and bruises, aches and pains. He thinks it's a nasty game. I am not going to be the person to dissuade him. Don't get me wrong: I love the game and I have loved my career, but I wouldn't want my son to have to put up with and experience what I have been through. While there is much that is good about my sport, it is also true that football can be very tribal, aggressive and often abusive.

I would go as far as to say that football has almost become the biggest religion in the world. People follow their team to the ends of the earth with a passion and desire that is sometimes bordering on insane. This is awesome for us as players because their support keeps our clubs in business. It lifts our spirits through tough matches and tough times. But with the good comes the bad, and it can be terrible for us as players because when it gets nasty, it can become personal. I usually find it easier to deal with the comments I receive on the pitch, because the fans that day are in direct opposition to my team, so I know to expect their hostility and see it as being more directed at my team than at me. It is the arbitrary comments that I receive in the street, or on social media, that are much harder to handle. The illogical and irrational way that football fans can categorise players because they play for a certain club is just beyond me. Having played for Burnley means that anything I ever say or do will be 'typical Dingle scum' according to one Blackburn fan. What the hell is that? It's crazy, that's what.

It is official. Northampton have concluded their most influential signing of the season. No, it's not me; it's Steve, the new chef. I cannot tell you how much of a difference this guy has made to our working life. The old chef was in no doubt as to the fruits of his labour when he told us what was on offer.

'What's for dinner, chef?'

'I'm sorry lads, it's . . .'

The guy would apologise before we'd even seen it, let alone tasted it. Steve, on the other hand, is performing minor miracles on a daily basis. We thought he'd been given a new limitless fund and found new suppliers, but no, it was the same budget and the same shop. The only difference was that he had some creativity in his work and he used his left-overs to create a salad bar that changed on a daily basis. It is awesome. Even the most reserved of palates is being tempted into trying some new dishes and new flavours. Instead of boiled-to-death chicken and boulder-weight spuds, we're being treated to minted lamb, Cajun chicken and, every once in a while, bangers and mash.

Better meals make a huge difference to the dynamic of the squad's interaction, too. Because the food is so good, every-one wants to stay every day to eat lunch together, and they'll do it with a smile on their face. This change of setting means that the content of our conversation changes, usually to rather more personal things, or political or current affairs, and you get lads revealing a lot more of themselves to each other. This increases the connection of the squad one to another, tightens the bond that is going to be vital if we are to be successful. If we do get promoted this year then I think that Steve, the best training ground chef I have ever encoun-tered in my career, should be at the front of the open-top bus around the town. If we don't, then he should pay for my subs at Weight Watchers next year.

Speaking of good food, Gem and I met up with some of our Burnley friends for a spot of Christmas dinner in Manchester. We ate with Graham Alexander, now the manager of Fleetwood Town, and his wife Karen; Steven Jordan, now at Dunfermline Athletic in Scotland, and his wife Katy; and Michael Duff, still at Burnley, and his wife Jess. We had a great time and a good catch-up, but afterwards both Gem and I had pangs of longing to be back at Burnley.

This is very abnormal for me. Gem calls me 'The Littlest Hobo', because I wander from club to club, making new friends and dropping old ones off with very little emotion; it's just the way that life as a footballer is. This is the only time when leaving a club has had a lasting impact on me. We loved it there. I would happily have stayed there for the rest of my career, so much so that I tried to have discussions with Eddie Howe and Paul Fletcher about having a dual role at the club, as Burnley is the site of the inaugural campus for the University College of Football Business.

It is an interesting initiative where they roll out courses on the specifics of running a football club, an industry that is completely different to any other. They had been asking me to get more involved with it and I went in as a visiting lecturer one day to share my experiences of the football world. I really enjoyed it and thought that I might be able to tie in some kind of role with them alongside being a member of the squad. I hoped it might give a double justification for the club to keep me on, not to mention being an opportunity for me to earn the £2500 per week that Gem and I were hopeful for. That would still have been a near 70 per cent pay cut on my previous contract with the club, but alas it wasn't to be. All good things must come to an end, but at least the friendships that we made don't have to. I can see this group gathering in 30 years' time and still reminiscing about our heyday at Turf Moor. Though I have to say that I hope we'll have one or two more anecdotes to share by then, because I don't know how many more times I can hear the story about Stevie Jordan putting Beasty to sleep outside a London restaurant.

Christmas Day was actually better than I'd expected. I

managed to spend Christmas morning at home with Gem and my three beautiful kids. It is actually the first time in ten years that Fran has spent Christmas Day with us, which was awesome. I had to leave for London shortly after lunch, so we had a special Christmas breakfast instead of dinner. I love the excitement and the gratitude that the kids show on Christmas Day. There are few better moments in life than when your child's eyes light up as they open a gift that they've been longing for.

On the other hand, you know you are getting old when your presents start to become practical. I don't know which is worse: the fact that I got Gem a slow cooker and an electric blanket, or the fact that they were exactly what she wanted? An initialled onesie for me next year, no doubt. Afterwards, Gem took the kids over to her auntie's and they all had dinner with her side of the family and I dropped off Fran with her mum while I carried on down to Kingston upon Thames to meet the lads at a Holiday Inn and spend Christmas night there.

This is one of the small sacrifices that you have to make as a footballer, and it is made a lot easier when you win the game the following day. However, it is made much worse when you don't even get to play the next day. On Boxing Day morning we awoke to a fresh fall of crisp, white snow. In the breakfast room the boys were chatting about the prospects of us playing at all. This would normally be done in low whispers, not wanting to convey any excitement or happiness that the fixture may be off. Today it was loud and in the open, because everyone to a man was annoyed that this game might be postponed. With another fixture in a couple of days, there would be no impromptu day/night out to look forward to, and the justification for abandoning our families the night before would have been lost. This was just, well, thoroughly inconvenient.

The confirmation came through that we were indeed heading back up the road without so much as getting our trainers dirty, never mind our boots, and our fixture list got compacted just that little bit more. The weather was causing murders, not least with the traffic, but I made my way back up north to salvage what was left of the festive period with my family.

CHAPTER 18

MORTIFIED

There are only two days to go before I am officially unemployed once more. I had placed my trust in Aidy to look after the contract situation and hadn't felt the need to harangue him about it, but it is getting a little close to the wire now. After a very brief conversation to check that he does want to keep me at the club, he would still be at liberty to just leave me high and dry should he so desire. However, he once more told me not to worry, and that all was in hand. When he got back to me later on, I was expecting to hear that the deal was all ready for me to come in and sign at training the next day. What I actually heard was something that made me a little nervous.

Apparently, there was no way that I could play on New Year's Day due to the timing of the paperwork. That being the case, Aidy thought it would be good for me to spend a few days at home with the family rather than traipse to training and back and to a game I can't play in. Had this been a match I was due to miss because of a suspension, I would have been delighted at the news. Because it was possibly the gaffer seeing if his team could cope without me, I was far from it. Not wanting to alarm her, I told Gem about it in the way it was relayed to me, so that it sounded like a favour and not an unbelievably precarious situation.

The next couple of days were horrible. I couldn't help but run through the worst-case scenarios over and over. What if Aidy has changed his mind about me? What if the chairman has just said no to Aidy's request? What if Aidy gets the sack? I've burned my bridges at York and I won't have anywhere to go; I will be royally buggered. I'm usually very good at times of uncertainty or doubt. I have this ability to box things off mentally and come back to them when necessary, but I couldn't get a hold of this one.

One thing that has been a blessing over these past three months has been Gem's new line of work. I think she has a similar mentality to me, inasmuch as when she decides to commit to something, she gives it 100 per cent for the duration. She has definitely shown me this in our marriage. She has recently shown it in her new job as a stylist for Stella & Dot, a jewellery company. You earn solely from commission and have to organise parties and events at which to show and sell your wares. It's one of those pyramid sales companies, where you employ other stylists for your team who you mentor, and you then gain a percentage of their sales, too. The amount of work that Mrs C has put into it recently has seen her get promoted twice in consecutive months. This means that she receives a greater percentage of her sales and those of her team. It's been going so well that this month Gem earned almost as much as I did, which is great news. It gave us a bit of disposable income with which to buy Christmas presents and the banquet of food that is mandatory for the festive period. My TV appearances have slowed down this month, so without Gem's wage we would have been buggered.

New Year was a quiet, forlorn affair. We were in bed by ten and I was woken by the fireworks. I went outside and sat on my front doorstep to watch the displays that could be seen across the valley. Another year gone, a new year had begun. What will it have in store for me? For us? I had high hopes for 2012, because I think I was caught up in all that Olympic Games hype. When I think about it realistically, what was there for me to have high hopes about?

A year ago I had just been bombed by Burnley in the Championship, and then bombed by Preston in League 1 and had to accept a place at Northampton, rock bottom of the Football League. What on earth was exciting about that? I suppose I had convinced myself that it couldn't get any worse, not so much that it was going to get any better. Here I am, a year on, and it may well have just got worse. Not only am I still at Northampton, but they could possibly have just bombed me as well. I am football's Mururoa Atoll – managers test their incendiary devices on me and I just take it. I might give Kim Jong-un a call; he would probably pay me a decent wage to be his whipping boy. Actually, he probably wouldn't.

It's Thursday 3 January and my third day of unemployment. I am in the gaffer's office, waiting for him to finalise the terms of my contract at Northampton with the chairman, David Cardoza. It is a little unnerving, considering they've had six weeks to sort it out. Aidy reassured me that there wouldn't be a problem, that he would get me the terms that we had agreed in our prior conversations, but I am beginning to think that it's not going to be so straightforward.

The crux of the matter is that I am in an extremely vulnerable position. I had placed my complete trust in Aidy from the off. I hadn't pestered him about the terms, about signing an agreement or anything to validate my position, because I wanted to show a level of trust that warranted reciprocation. I wanted to show that money wasn't the be-all and end-all for me, although it is important. I wanted to show that I was focused on football.

Unfortunately, however noble and principled I felt I was being, this approach had done nothing to force the hand of the football club. They, like every other club out there, appear to have adopted an 'out of sight, out of mind' attitude towards this issue. Now that I am out of contract, with absolutely no other options out there because of how I've gone about things, Northampton, and Mr Cardoza in particular, have me by the short and curlies. More than that, he actually has my plums in his palm and it is up to him how hard he squeezes them. I am completely at his mercy.

When Aidy came into the office, I could tell by the look on his face that everything wasn't going as planned. Knowing exactly where the power lies, the chairman has set out the terms and they are non-negotiable: an 18-month deal on £1200 per week, plus £100 per appearance, no fuel allowance and accommodation on a 'when necessary' basis. Take it or leave it.

I am not going to lie, I was absolutely raging. I had committed to Aidy without hesitation because I know what he is capable of, and I know what this squad can achieve. But to join the club had been a tough decision, as I told him at the time, because York was only 45 minutes from my house, which meant that I could be with my family every day. Although money is important to me, not least because of that family that I need to support, I am at a stage in my career where I am not chasing every last pound; my priorities are different to what they were ten years ago. I want my wife and children to be settled and happy, and I want to be there to enjoy what is such an amazing time of life when the kids are this age.

My biggest concern over moving to Northampton was the cost in time. Now that I am able to drive again, it takes three hours to get there in the morning and two and a half to get back in the afternoons. This means that I barely ever see my children for most of the week, and I get a Sunday with them only if we don't have a midweek game. If I am going to give up all of that, it has to be worth it financially. Yet what I was being offered meant that I would be taking home less than I was on at York. My petrol costs alone were in excess of £1000 per month. This contract means I will need to do more TV work each month to guarantee that we can pay the bills, so I get even less time to spend with the family.

What a royal fucking mess, because there is absolutely nothing I can do about it now. I am just going to have to deal with it. I didn't whinge or have a hissy fit; I smiled, signed and got on with training. What else can I do? There is nothing to gain from any other reaction. At least they didn't renege on the length of the contract, which would have been the icing on the cake. I am just going to have to do all I can to make sure that we are successful. If we get promoted, there's always a chance that this contract might be improved after all.

I'm not sure I should tell Mrs C exactly what the terms are; she's not been best pleased at my decision to move back to Northampton when I could have stayed at York. It effectively makes her live like a single mum for the duration of the season, and now I need to tell her she'll be doing that for less money than we were expecting. Maybe that's a conversation that will have to wait.

I have just experienced the single most embarrassing moment of my life. I have been doing co-commentary for ITV on the African Cup of Nations. It's a great gig. I get to chat about football for 90 minutes and I get paid for doing so – brilliant. It's not actually as simple as it seems. There is an art to commentary, especially on televised matches. The commentator needs to be able to maintain interest in what can often be dull and lifeless encounters, while ensuring he doesn't talk for talking's sake.

There is also an art to co-commentary, as I am rapidly finding out. Everyone can see what has happened, they are watching the same pictures as you and they have been guided through the play by the main commentator. The last thing they then need is for you to repeat what they have just seen and what they have already heard. The commentator verbalises *what* just happened, my job is to explain to everyone *why* it happened. It is vital but tough to keep that explanation concise, because play continues. What this means is that you need to see the reasons for what just occurred and then convey them before any other action of note takes place. If you don't, then the main commentator will understandably have no qualms about cutting you off mid-sentence.

It's a really enjoyable role. It is much easier to do this when you are actually up in the stands at a match. You can see the whole pitch and, more importantly, what is happening off the ball in order to pre-empt problems that may arise. However, with this tournament we are commentating 'off tube'. That means we are trying to evaluate the match from the same pictures that the audience is seeing. And the cameras always concentrate on the ball rather than anything else that might be going on around the periphery. Not only that, but the feed is controlled by the host broadcasters, in this case South African TV, so we don't know what replays and camera angles are coming, until they actually show up on our screens. It's all very ad hoc.

So, I'm sitting in a little sweatbox sound booth with Peter Drury, commentating on Ghana versus Burkina Faso after a long day of meetings and travelling. The room is so small that we're virtually in each other's lap, but I suppose it's all that's necessary for two men, two TVs, two mikes and head-phones. Because I had a game the night before, I was very tired, so I plied myself with coffee by the gallon in order to keep myself awake and *compos mentis* for this job. That was my big mistake.

About 20 minutes into the first half, I started to need the toilet. Okay, I have to hold it until half time. You can't just bob out to the loo when you are doing comms, especially in such a small room, as the noise of me getting up and the door opening and closing would echo across however many million houses that are watching. Thirty minutes in and I'm starting to get a bit of bellyache as my bladder reaches maxi-mum capacity. Forty minutes in and I'm hotfooting underneath the table like I'm practising the *Riverdance*. It's all I can do to keep my mind off the fact that my bladder is about to explode. Forty-five minutes gone and the fourth official holds up the board to signal how much injury time there will be, and how soon I can make my escape . . . SIX MINUTES!

I can't do it. I can't last. I can't speak. I can't keep still. These are the longest minutes of my life. Forty-seven minutes in and I feel a little dribble down the inside of my leg. Oh shit. No, hold on, you can do it. Forty-eight minutes and I suffer a minor convulsion; my body is malfunctioning and it can't understand why I am still sitting in a soundproofed box of self-inflicted pain. Forty-nine minutes and a little patch appears on the inside of my jeans. Oooohh shit, these are stonewash jeans; that patch is going to stand out like a beacon of incontinence.

Finally the ref puts the whistle to his lips and, before he has finished blowing it, I am out of my seat. Peter tries to calmly and professionally give the link to the break as I am yanked back into my seat. Aaargh, take the bloody headphones off, IT'S COMING OUT! I sling them on the table and crash out of the door as I feel the warm flow of urine gush down my leg. I clatter through the toilet door and wrestle with the button fly. A bloody button fly at a moment like this! By the time I wrench my jeans down, it's too late, I'm done. I'm standing in the toilets at the ITV studios with two-tone jeans on, one leg stonewashed, the other piss-drenched.

What the hell am I supposed to do now? I can't even make a run for it – I've got about ten minutes before I have to get back in the sweatbox and do the second-half commentary. I have no change of clothes and, even if I did, I would have to walk through the building with its bright halogen lights, steam coming off one leg. Then I had a thought: maybe ten minutes will be long enough for me to dry my jeans under the blowers. Oh no, I am royally screwed. We're in the sound dub section of the building, so there are no hand dryers! I can't even leave the toilets; I'm going to be stuck here forever.

Hold on a minute! I had a mini brain wave. It was a long shot, but it was all I could think of. I took my jeans and drawers off, threw the drawers in the bin and stuck my jeans in the sink. If I can't make my jeans dry, I'm just going to have to make them all wet. I soaked them through so that they were the same shade of blue from top to bottom, then tried to put them back on. Have you ever tried to put on wet jeans? It's almost impossible. After a struggle, I managed to get them on, tucked myself in and bowled back through to the sound booth as bold as brass.

I have never been as paranoid in my life as I was through-out that entire second 45 minutes. Peter never mentioned anything, but I was convinced that I smelt like the local tramp. As the game wore on, my jeans started to dry out. The colour was changing from top to bottom like a pair of dip-dyes. I squeezed myself further under the desk until I could barely move. At the final whistle, I pretended to jot down notes about the game in my folder, desperate for Peter to leave so that I could get out of my chair. Thankfully, he was in a rush and left quite quickly, but nowhere near as fast as I did when I made a run for my car.

I can't believe that just happened. I have never wet myself without alcohol before. I hope this isn't the first sign of old age. Driving home half-naked, I just had to tell someone. You know you're in love when that someone is your wife. I don't know if she found it as funny as she did revolting, but the first thing she said was: 'Get it in your book.'

So here it is. Clarke 'Piss-Pants' Carlisle. Thirty-three years of age. Mortified.

— CHAPTER 19 —

INFINITY 2012

I have had to admit defeat. It is one of my biggest annoyances in life when I fail to complete something, but my university course has become one commitment too many. I have had to put my final year back by 12 months; I just don't have the time to commit to it. I was hoping that I would be able to box off one weekend each month to concentrate on my course, but it just doesn't work like that. Some of the modules this semester require daily analysis. For example, you have to commit a couple of hours each night to assess the effect of your advertisement campaign and foot traffic across your blog site. I was only just managing to find the time to write the blog, never mind checking every night to see how many people are reading it and why.

I am not going to give up on it altogether. I have discussed it with my tutors and I can pick up the course again in September, which will hopefully be when I have far fewer extra-curricular commitments to fulfil. I have been discussing with Gem why it is that I can't just put the course down completely. The truth is that it is entirely because of what people will think, and that I fear they will see me as having failed. I don't want anyone to think that.

But the reality is that my TV work portfolio is steadily growing, and I am already in talks about a permanent job at a major broadcaster. So I have to ask myself: what purpose is this course actually fulfilling at this time other than personal satisfaction? I believe it is a good course to give me a general overview of the journalism industry, but I am now quite clear about what area of that world I want to be in. At least I have the consolation that this journey hasn't hit the buffers completely. I can cope with that; I have lost the battle, but the war is still ongoing.

We've just had another great couple of days' training. We were in the gym yesterday on the exercise bikes and I began to get a bit carried away. I'm not sure if other athletes have this kind of thought process when they're working out, but when I got going on that bike, I became my own worst coach. We were supposed to be doing a warm-down, but I started to get into it. I can never do half measures with anything, so I began turning my legs over faster and faster, and this crazy notion came into my head that I could become a cyclist. Perhaps it was because in the last few months I've read the book about Eddy Merckx, *Half Man, Half Bike*, and Tyler Hamilton's *The Secret Race*, that I was thinking in this way. I really do fancy myself on the bike. At Burnley I broke records on the bike for distances and so I let my mind run free with the idea.

I wonder if other athletes dabble in a different sport and think that they could do it quite easily? I'd bet many do, as there are plenty I know who have the confidence to think they can take on any challenge. With cycling, especially if you gave me a dose of 'Edgar Allan Poe', I began to believe that I've got the ability and suddenly I'd be the leader of the peloton.

We were given a few days off, but before you can enjoy them there is always standard procedure: to get a bit of time off you must be punished. It's really pissed me off for 17 years now. When we went out to train, the gaffer decided that he was going to beast us before we had our break. We started with activation, then moved on to the weights. I have to confess, they're not for me. Only once in my career have I got into upper-body weights, and that was with Alan 'Mahonovich' Mahon. He'd come up with a routine of supersets of bicep curls, shoulder presses and upright rows. I was getting pretty decent after a few weeks of doing the same routine, getting up to 30kg dumbbells. Some might expect a big guy like me to be better at this, but because I've never worked on this aspect I don't have any natural weight-throwing strength, unlike Shittu and Bayo.

After we'd completed our gym work, it was time to go outside for ten box-to-box runs that turned into 12 on a pitch that resembled a bog, then eight star runs around the centre circle. We finished off with 20-yard doggies with a bench at each end that we had to jump over and then do two press-ups. We had three minutes of those, then a break, then two minutes, break, one minute. Just as we got to the end of that little lot, Aidy said he thought we could do more, so we did a further four minutes.

That is Aidy all over. It's not the physical work that he's really interested in, it's the psychological and mental aspects. He wants to know that we're mentally tough enough and that he won't break us. Even on the boxes, he told us we'd be doing ten and then when we'd crossed the line on the tenth he shouted for us to do two more, just to see if we could gear ourselves up to do it again and to check who will put in the effort and who will throw in the towel. It's a measure of this group that the boys did it, to a man. You really enjoy the shower afterwards, knowing that you've put in a good shift, it's all in the bank. I actually found that I got faster towards the end, knowing that the day off was near.

Afterwards we went into a thinking session, doing a SWOT appraisal of ourselves, and this epitomises Aidy's approach. He doesn't just want dummies, who are told what to do, where to go and when. He wants an interactive squad, a thinking squad; he wants players who analyse the team. A SWOT session is when you assess Strengths, Weaknesses, Opportunities and Threats. So for me, my main strength would be aerial ability and my main weakness would be my lack of mobility. This means that there is an opportunity to exploit me if you put a pacy and mobile striker up against me, while my main threat would come from attacking the ball at set pieces.

Understanding your strengths and weaknesses can make a huge difference to your game, because it enables you to judge when you have the ability to be elaborate and when to keep something basic and play the percentages. And when it comes to our weaknesses, Aidy doesn't leave it at that. He always impresses on us that these are only things that we are not good at yet, 'yet' being the operative word. He is constantly encouraging us to focus on improvement: 'If we all improve one per cent individually, we improve eleven per cent as a team.' I love that attitude; I love the way he addresses our mindsets. We're not allowed to think 'I can't do some-thing', it's 'I can't do it yet', and that approach creates a dynamic of forward thinking and progress, because we end up believing we will be able to do it at some point, or do it better at least.

We then had to analyse how we would beat ourselves, as though we were an opposing team. It was incredibly interesting. The lads were honest without being hypercritical. We were given a compendium of statistics on our performances to date and it just made me think of 'lies, damn lies and statistics'. There are some stats that you really don't want your squad latching on to, because they can create negative thinking. One that came through was the fact that Northampton have drawn three matches and lost six after going a goal behind. Now if that fact were to become embedded in your squad's minds, then psychologically you are screwed, because if you go into a game and concede in the first five minutes, then the reaction could easily be: 'Oh well, that's it. We're not going to win now, the best we can do is draw.' Subconsciously that's been drilled into the brain, and it can lead to very negative reactions in certain scenarios, putting the team in a fairly hopeless position.

The same logic applies when considering the opposition, too. If we were playing a side that has gone on to win every game when they have scored first, as a manager I don't think you should furnish your team with that fact. The way you dress it up is to say that the first goal is very important, that the starting tempo to the game has to be controlled by us, and then to not panic should anything go against the plan. That way there isn't a sense of the result being a foregone conclusion at any stage of the game.

There are so many areas of management that can cause similar problems; there are fine lines to be walked so that the delicate psyche of the modern-day footballer isn't disturbed.

And here I am, mulling this over back in the Northampton Travelodge, living the superstar lifestyle. Where did it all go right? A few years ago, I was staying in The Grove, and even a few months ago I was being put up in plush London hotels, but now it's a £19-a-night gaff with wobbly beds, wonky shelves, and £5.48 for my dinner. Luxury!

I have played some matches in terrible conditions, but tonight was by far the most ridiculous game of professional football that I have ever played. Away at Aldershot can be a taxing fixture at the best of times. It is a classic lower league ground, terraced on three sides with the old shed-style corrugated roofs. The ground looks old and tired, a lot like me, when you can actually see it. But because the snow was falling so heavily it meant that visibility was reduced to about half a pitch. As I've mentioned, my eyesight is failing in clear daylight; so I'd got absolutely no chance of seeing anything in this. The snow-fall was so bad that it hurt your eyes to look into the wind, your eyeballs were being battered by icy shards and it was a triumph to see anything through squinted eyes.

We walked out on to the pitch before kick-off with complete certainty that the game would be called off. We brought a ball out with us and tried to kick it between us. It was almost impossible. Snow clumped around the ball and made it into some misshapen dodecahedron that rolled erratically from side to side and bobbled unpredictably. Surely playing on this was going to be a health hazard? Aidy had other ideas, and when Aidy wants, Aidy gets. The referee was persuaded into playing the fixture, even though the lines weren't visible. The groundsmen were desperately trying to burn the pitch markings on to the pitch, but no sooner had they walked ten yards away than the snow had covered their tracks. I haven't played in conditions like this since I was ten years old, and I cried then.

We kicked off in relative disbelief that the game was going ahead and I wasn't at all surprised when we went 1-0 down early on. We could barely see the ball, never mind judge where it was going or how fast. About 15 minutes in, an orange ball was introduced into the game. Where the hell had they been hiding it? It completely changed things for me because I could actually see what we were playing with. My only concern from there on in was trying to keep my footing while moving around the pitch.

We won the game 2-1, which included my first goal since my return to Northampton. It was the usual centre-half's goal, a header from a corner just two yards out. I'm lethal from that distance. I would have celebrated if I had any feeling in my body. I couldn't afford to expend the energy; it was all being channelled into ensuring I didn't get frostbite. I would have been far more critical of both the ref and Aidy had we lost the game, as it was utterly ludicrous to play in that, but with three points under our belts it was a shot in the arm for our promotion push and another triumph over relative adversity.

I didn't thaw out until we were about half an hour from Northampton. It was only at this point that I realised it felt like my foot was wet. Taking my trainer off, I saw that I had a huge gash on one of my toes and my trainer was drenched in blood. I hadn't noticed it before because it was numb due to the cold and it hadn't bled because of the lack of blood flow that I suffer from. There must be something quite seriously wrong with my circulation; I think I need to get it properly checked out.

We were supposed to have a day off today, but instead we went to visit one of our team-mates in hospital. Alex Nicholls has had an absolutely torrid time this year. In the first month of the season, he suffered a double fracture of his leg when he collided with the goalkeeper in the process of scoring a goal. This would be traumatic enough for any player on its own, but the series of setbacks that followed were enough to drive a person over the edge.

After having been operated on when a rod was put in his leg, he developed an infection that refused to go away. He had to have the wound cleaned out several times until it was ascertained that it was actually the metalwork inside his leg that was causing the infection in the first place. He then had to have that removed and one of those huge contraptions fitted to his leg which looked like a Meccano set, with four rods fixed directly to his bones and protruding out and attached to the brace. This was at three points up his leg and all bolted together. It was a mess, physically and metaphorically.

This had all happened over the course of five months, during which he had tried to start exercising again, only to be repeatedly knocked back by infection after infection, one so severe that he was almost delirious with it. It has been so tough to try to greet him and keep his spirits up each day. Knowing what I do from my injury way back when, I have tried to keep asking about his capacity to cope without badgering or reminding him of the severity of his situation. He has just had another (hopefully final) operation and we travelled down en masse to his hospital in London.

It is impossible to make someone feel like they are still part of the team when they are not with you each day. The loneliness of long-term injury can be devastating. Imagine his surprise when he came down from his hospital bed and saw 20-odd of his mates all ready to take him out for lunch. It was a brilliant idea from the skipper, and Nicho seemed quite emotional at the gesture. This showed me just how close this group of guys is. There were no complaints or dissenting voices about giving up our day off; everyone was unanimous in their support of the visit and in their support of Nicho. It really was a beautiful thing. It was impossible not to reflect on your own situation and be grateful for your blessings, for your health and all of the things that you take for granted.

It seems that the thing I thought was going to be the answer to my problem of 'time' has served only to make it worse. Now that I am back on the road, I expected to have so much more free time to have meetings and see the family, but it hasn't really worked out that way. Before now the decision would be made for me whether I got back up north of an evening, purely because of the train schedule. If I wasn't free to leave by late afternoon, then there was no chance of me making it home for any useful period of time, so I would stay in the hotel and get some work done, or organise meetings in my vicinity.

Now that I can just jump in the car and be home in a little more than two hours, there is rarely a reason to stay in Northampton other than it being the night before a game. This has resulted in two things. Firstly, I am not scheduling any meetings nor am I writing any of the tens of thousands of words that are necessary to fill this book. Secondly, and more importantly, I am actually upsetting the children more with this new routine of being at home for an hour and disappearing before they wake up in the morning. 'Out of sight, out of mind' is a very true proverb when it comes to the minds of children, and they cope far better when I am away for a block period of time, and then return for the same. This Scarlet Pimpernel act is causing them a lot more distress when they wake up to find that I've disappeared again, especially for our two-year-old, Honey May. Gem has had to call me in the morning when Honey wakes up because the poor girl is inconsolable at the fact that I'm not there. She will calm down only when she has heard my voice on the phone and been reassured that I'll be home soon.

This is not the best way to start your day, for either Gem or me. The only consolation is the end of the conversation when a 'love off' ensues. I will say 'I love you' to Honey May and she will reply with 'I love you more', and so begins a competition that puts a big smile on my face. Marley has actually coined a new phrase for us all in this. It began when Gem started to put numerical values on her love, which went back and forth increasingly as Marley's knowledge of numbers grew. One day Gem told him: 'Well, I love you infinity.'

'What's infinity?' asked Marley.

'It's the biggest value that you can ever get; it goes on forever and doesn't stop.'

Marley pondered this information for a while before finally replying: 'Well, I love you infinity 2012, that's the biggest EVER.'

We had a chuckle at his logic and the more I thought about it, the more I liked the term: 'Infinity 2012'. It has a certain ring to it. If I ever form a company then I know what I'm going to name it, but I'll have to make sure Marley gets his copyright fee.

CHAPTER 20

ON THE MOVE AGAIN

D o you ever get that feeling that someone is watching over you? The more that I look back over my life, the more convinced I am that my family and I are a blessed group of people. I explained earlier how tough it had been to even try to sell our house, but then this guy comes and tasks us with getting out of there as soon as humanly possible. This would have been perfect if we had the resources to instantly up and leave, buy a new property and get in there straight away. However we don't, and his purchase plan has made it even harder. He wants to rent the place off us for 18 months and then buy it at the end. This means that we are going to have to either rent a property ourselves for the same period, or find another vendor who is willing to commit to the same agreement. One more spanner in the works is that this guy can't afford a deposit, so we can't realise any of our capital in the house to place a deposit on a property ourselves. We are going to have to find an incredibly generous, risk-taking vendor, or tens of thousands of pounds.

I had been deliberating on this conundrum for weeks, months even, and it was driving me insane. Finding a seller who is willing to work with these restrictions is nigh-on impossible, and there is no way that we can magic up a pot of cash. So one day I came home from training to tell Gem about the conclusion I had come to: we just can't buy a new house, not yet. We are going to have to put a hold on our pursuit of happiness until it is stress-free, and we had to recognise that this would probably mean a wait of three or four years.

Gem had been away all weekend in London at a conference for her business. She had benefited from three days of continual positive speaking and thinking, and she had been inspired by many of the talks and one quote in particular from Richard Branson: 'Have faith in yourself; think "yes" not "no"; live life to the full and never give up.' She was ready to try to share some of this new-found enthusiasm with me when I rained all over her parade with my thoughts. This was sod's law. It was usually me convincing Gem to take a step of faith, to take a risk and believe that we could get through the situation together. Yet now, the one time that she came home with all guns blazing, ready to march on into the unknown, I burst her bubble before she could even open her mouth.

She shared this thought with me and I realised how vitally important we are to each other. We are a team. When one is down the other helps them up, when one is hesitant the other helps them forward, and when one feels loved, we both feel loved. I was about to throw in the towel on the whole venture, but Gem took the towel, span me around and whipped me on the backside with it instead.

I'm not sure how to describe what happened to me this week, other than I had an 'episode'. My depression took a hold of me with a terrifying grip and it's pretty much my own fault. The past few days I have been completely unable to function. I am consumed by lethargy and just want to sleep, all of the time. I didn't get out of bed for two days other than to go to the toilet. I haven't eaten more than three meals in the week and I haven't answered my phone to anyone other than Gem. It is an utterly horrendous feeling. I can't bring myself to talk to anyone, let alone actually see them.

It began when I drove to training and couldn't bring myself to get out of the car. The drive to training from my hotel is probably about three minutes long, and I could feel my eyes being forced closed throughout the entire journey. After sitting in the car park for about half an hour, I just turned around and went home.

I really should have seen it coming. The crazy thoughts that I was having over the New Year were a clear indication that something wasn't right. My sleep has been out of kilter, too. I had started to stay up really late at nights, unable to sleep even though I was shattered. During the day I could feel my body wanting to shut down, to just fall asleep there and then. It wasn't tiredness as such; instead it felt as if I was switching off. It was the strangest feeling. I had also started to think unreasonably about things that Gem said. A simple question like 'What are you doing later?' would make my mind spiral off into thoughts of a lack of trust and that she was grilling me.

It was only as I got back into bed that morning that I realised what was going on. I started to question myself: why couldn't I go to work? Why couldn't I face anyone? Why was I feeling so low? Then I remembered that I had stopped taking my fluoxetine some seven or eight weeks ago. I had run out not long after moving down to Northampton from York and kept forgetting to ask my new doctor for a prescription. This was partly due to the fact that I was a little embarrassed about revealing my depression to yet another person, and partly due to the fact that I hoped I was now 'cured' and could cope without it.

After a couple of weeks, I still felt okay and figured I'd have a go at being 'clean' for a while. I continued to feel okay until, whammy, I fell over the edge. I texted Aidy to tell him I was struggling and I needed to see him. I drove back around to the club and he was outside the ground. I started to tell him how I was feeling and I just broke down. Eventually I explained what was going on and Aidy was fantastic. He told me to go and do whatever it was that I needed to do. I told him the first thing was to get another prescription, then I would have to go home, speak to my wife and speak to my counsellor.

So he sent me home for a few days and told me that he would explain it to the lads, saying that I would be coming back on Monday morning ready to work. And so I did. I must confess that I still wasn't feeling fine and dandy on Monday morning, but I felt a whole lot better than I did that Thursday.

This situation has really shocked me. It scared me how simple it was to lose sight of maintaining my mental state. It scared me how dramatic it can be to fall off the edge of reason. Even with my prior understanding of dealing with depression, it still managed to creep up and hit me with a hammer. I can only say that I'm glad I had an inkling as to what was going on, otherwise I could have gone into freefall.

I was also lucky that I have a manager who is open to matters of the mind. Aidy said that he didn't have any first-hand knowledge of depression, but had experienced it with someone close to him and knew how bad it can be. I know that many other managers wouldn't be so sympathetic. It transpires that he told the press and the lads that I had flu, which is interesting. I wonder if that was just because it was a simple explanation which needed no elaboration, or whether he thought he was protecting me from the intrusion that revealing the truth might possibly cause?

When I did manage to get out of the car the following Monday morning, I was greeted with jeers and heckles: 'You must be the new guy? Nice to meet you.'

'It's all right for some. Have a nice week off?'

'I'm gonna get "Southend flu" next time too.'

You can always rely on a group of guys to be sympathetic to your ailments.

A few days after my 'return', Bayo enquired as to my actual whereabouts the previous week. My depression is not something that I want to be covert about, so I told B in some detail what happened. He was amazed. Not by my honesty – I think we've got to a place where we would expect nothing less from each other – but by the reality of something that he hadn't come across before.

He said to me: 'I've heard about things like this before but, when I see it happening with *you*, when I hear *you* saying that you can't get out of the car, it makes it real.'

The revelation brought us closer and served to further strengthen a bond that we had already made. One of the greatest lies that depression creates for the sufferer is that people will react or treat them negatively if they reveal the nature of their thoughts and feelings. Utter tripe. Honesty conveys a level of trust that will almost certainly be reciprocated, and when that trust is placed in a person who loves and respects you, your vulnerability just endears you to them more.

B's reaction was indicative of virtually every player with whom I had broached the subject. In a surprising number of cases, it would lead to some kind of admission of similar feelings or knowledge of a similar situation. It is really very alarming how many people have suffered or are suffering from a level of depression and haven't been able to talk to anyone about it, or known who to talk to. A lot of people have experienced similar feelings but had no knowledge of what was going on, which is also very troubling.

There is a distinct lack of awareness of, and education about, depression and mental health issues. This has to change. The consciousness of the nation, not to say the world, has been woken by the advances in technology and research. Every mother is now aware of the symptoms of meningitis, measles, anaphylactic reactions/shock and even the comparisons between breast milk and formula. The public's knowledge of cancers, from breast to testicular to prostate to melanoma, has expanded significantly since medical research has highlighted the potential triggers, symptoms and risks. People are taking food intolerance measures even when they are at no acknowledged risk, just in case.

Why, then, is there such a reluctance to acknowledge, raise awareness of and educate ourselves about an illness that is the most common cause of death for men aged 35 and under? If I said that 6000 people were going to die in the UK this year, but most of these deaths could be prevented by a simple conversation, you'd think I was mad. Over 6000 people will commit suicide this year, and a high percentage of them will be clinically depressed and they won't even know it or know what to do about it. Just tell someone, anyone, and then go and talk to your GP. The first conversation is the hardest; it gets easier and easier from there.

Well, we've only gone and done it. We have actually managed to find a property that Gem loves, is within our budget and has a vendor willing to take a chance. I can't bloody believe it. He will happily enter into a rental agreement simultaneous with the one on our property, but he would like the security of a ten per cent deposit in order to delay the completion for 18 months. The place is awesome as well. Our family have clubbed together to help us with the deposit, which we can repay when we sell our house. This is a wonderful day.

It gets even better, too. The weekend that we are supposed to be moving into the new house, I have an away fixture for Northampton. This means that Gem is going to have to do it all by herself. I'm only kidding – about Gem being on her own, that is. I definitely won't be there. Again, our family is pulling together to help as much as possible. Before now we've been able to use a removal service such as Pickfords, who will come into the house, box up everything and take it over to the new place for you.

This relocation cost is usually included as part of the contract when you sign for a new club. However, Northampton wouldn't agree to put that clause in my contract, because we weren't moving to within 30 miles of the club, which is one of the usual stipulations. So, because we'd always had this sort of thing paid for in the past, we'd never found out how much this actually costs. When they came to price up the move, they told us that they would charge us £2500 for the job. That'll be the end of that idea, then.

Our van problem was solved by my brother and, bizarrely, the guy who is buying our house. He is so keen to get us out that he is renting a van and is going to shift all the gear with Gem. He is Roy, Robbie, Kevin and Steve all in one man – the ultimate Mr Keen. I'll be leaving one house on the Thursday and then coming home to a different house on the Sunday, which will feel very strange.

I truly hope that this is the last move for us. We've picked a quiet village just in between York and Harrogate. It's perfect for Gem's family, who all live within 20 minutes of the new place, which is just how she wanted it. The school is better than Marley's old one, and it's a state school as well, saving us a small fortune in school fees. Last but probably most important, there are several great golf courses all around it. That's going to be vital for Marley's development, not that I'm pushing him.

Moving into this property isn't a step of faith, it's a veritable leap. We both know that in less than 18 months' time I will not be playing football. In fact, I probably won't be playing in 18 weeks' time, so we are placing great trust in my post-football career. We have discussed this over and over again, yet we always come to the same conclusion: if I apply myself to my second career with the same application and focus that I did with football, I will achieve infinitely more. All of the ingredients are there. I am married to a wonderful woman who supports me in all that I do. I have three beautiful children who I want to provide everything for. I have an excitement and a desire to make a difference, to make an impact and, most of all, to prove people wrong! What's the worst-case scenario? We lose both houses, I'll end up without a job and I'll have to start all over again – it's just a flesh wound.

CHAPTER 21

IS HE MENTAL?

I've done a few interviews with various media outlets this week because attention has returned to the issue of racism. The talk about the creation of a Black Players' Union which began last October has not gone away and lawyer Peter Herbert is banging the drum for all to hear. I couldn't think of anything worse. I have already illustrated that creating such an entity would instantly define 'us' and 'them'. It would cause division in the PFA, an organisation that has fought so hard for inclusivity in football for nearly four decades now.

What I will say on the topic, though, is that the meetings that have been ongoing at the union have highlighted certain issues. The player base we have is without doubt one of the most diverse workgroups in the world. The union itself also has a very high percentage of BME employees, far higher than the national average. Lower than average, though, are the number of BME players getting into coaching and management.

The other problem that has been highlighted is a discernable conflict of interest for the anti-discrimination organisations that exist in football. Because Kick It Out and Show Racism the Red Card are part-funded by the PFA, the Premier League, the Football League and the FA, or a combination of them all, there could be a reluctance for these organisations to be as vocal as is necessary when certain incidents occur, as their funding comes from bodies that might not want to deal with these issues full-on, or would prefer things to be handled as quietly as possible.

After several of these meetings, I have to pay credit to the likes of Jason Roberts and other players who have made a stand. Admittedly they made their stand on a platform that I wouldn't have chosen, but they felt it was the only way available to them to make their voices heard. I know that I have been extremely fortunate to have access to the places where I can get my point across, and not everybody has that. One thing that I don't think was widely acknowledged by many in the group was that the mechanism is already in place for players to have their voice heard within the union. That is what the management committee is for. Players can feed their opinions into people on the committee, and they then bring it to the discussion table. I'm just not sure how many lads know that this is how it works.

That's going to have to be something we change. There is no need to set up a separate body. The way to move forward is to get these opinions to the discussion tables within the union. They can then be discussed, and then a decision can be made that will serve the best interests of all of our members.

As if this wasn't enough, I've been getting battered on Twitter for using words that are too long. Why get abuse for using your vocabulary? I try to learn new words all of the time. Just because I don't have a degree in English Language doesn't mean that I can't try to learn new things. Why does it make you 'twattish' for wanting to better yourself? Well, at the risk of upsetting some weirdly concerned individuals out there, I'm going to continue my routine of trying to learn a new word every month, a pursuit I will undertake with alacrity.

The filming for my second documentary has taken me over to Germany this week, the first time I have ever been there. When the production team suggested that we head over there for three days, I laughed. I was sure there was absolutely no way that I could possibly get the time to do it at this stage of the season, and even if I had the time I couldn't see Aidy allowing it. Well, I was proved very wrong. Not only did the gaffer give me the time to go to Germany, but he also gave me an extra day off when I returned so that I could spend some time with Gem and the kids. This is why I chose to come here and work with him. I cannot envisage another manager in the land being so amenable.

The documentary is about depression and suicide in sport, a topic that I obviously have a great affinity with. I am working with the same company that produced the film *Is Football Racist?*, which I presented last year. When we went into our first discussion about the racism film, I also pitched my outline for this documentary. This was all months before the tragic suicide of Gary Speed, which only deepened my resolve to look into this issue.

I got on incredibly well with my last team. The executive producer, David Dehaney, is a brilliant man who exudes calm in what can be a very manic world. The producer was

Adam Jessel and the assistant producer was Donald Stewart. Adam was the most anxious man I have ever met, constantly fiddling and deliberating about what to do. But he was excellent at shaping the film and came up with some great ideas for the content. Don, a very cool, easy-going kind of guy who doesn't panic but just gets it done, was the perfect foil to him.

When I heard that Adam wasn't available for this second film, I was perturbed to say the least. I rang David several times to see if there was any way that we could change schedules or do something to get him involved, but alas, it wasn't to be. The person given the job of producing this film is Anna Keel. Before we got started, I felt that Anna had a lot to live up to, not only because I enjoyed working with Adam so much, but also because he produced an excellent film, one that I am proud to be associated with.

It took only a couple of shoots for me to realise that I had absolutely nothing to worry about. Anna is just as good as Adam at the job, if not better. I say that because we share a moment of hilarity in every shoot, and that makes it so pleasurable to work with her. She has absolutely no grounding in football whatsoever. She comes out with brilliant lines that expose her complete lack of knowledge of the terminology used in the game, but she says these things so innocently it is rather endearing. She also has a tendency to verbalise her thoughts, resulting in her having whole conversations with herself, which can be incredibly amusing to listen to. She too is a bit of a worrier, so having Don 'the fixer' alongside works perfectly well once again.

When you're dealing with such a serious, delicate and emotional topic, it would be easy for the whole atmosphere to become oppressive. What I have actually found is that going on this journey of discovery about depression has been incredibly cathartic. We have found time to laugh and smile at the most inappropriate of times. It made me think that this is what it might be like to work at a hospital, or in a funeral parlour, where you cannot be consumed by your work otherwise you would just be reduced to a complete wreck.

There was one time when I was talking to a young man about how his career in football had ended and what it meant to him as a person and the repercussions it had had on his life. He was getting really deep into the moment when, out of the corner of my eye, I saw Anna kneeling down and stroking the AstroTurf pitch. I wondered what the hell she was doing, just caressing the park like that. She told me afterwards that she had never felt turf before and thought it looked really fluffy, so she gave in to the urge to stroke it. I could probably have handled that, but then Don, who has followed football for decades, got drawn in as well and had a little fiddle. What the hell? Soon, pretty much the entire production team were on their hands and knees stroking a random AstroTurf pitch in the middle of London. Bizarre.

When you are walking around with a huge camera, it inevitably attracts the interest of the passing public. Whether people are young or old, rich or poor, quiet or loud, the camera draws them all in with its gravitational pull. Most people are generally polite and plain inquisitive, but not always.

While out in Germany we were taking some 'thinking' shots. This constitutes me sitting outside a café staring off into the distance looking all pensive and moody. While we were mid-shot, a local man sidled up to the camera and asked the crew what we were doing.

'We're filming a documentary.'

'Okay, what is it about?'

'Depression and mental health issues.'

Following the camera's line of sight, he looked over at me and pointed: 'Oh, is he mental?'

Brilliant. The guy had named that tune in one.

We had arranged to do a shoot at the 1860 Munich training ground. We got there and set up ready for the shoot when who should walk out of the dressing room but none other than Gabor Kiraly, my old team-mate from Burnley, and he still had those bloody rascal tracksuit bottoms on. I had no idea he was here. He was shortly followed by Moritz Volz, a guy who I had been on the PFA management committee with for a couple of years. This is one thing I love about football, it is a global community. I have travelled hundreds of miles from home and I end up bumping into two old mates – brilliant! Gem doesn't like it so much. I don't think we've been on a holiday yet where I haven't bumped into someone I know or have played against.

The trip was a great success with regard to the film. We got some valuable insight from the psychiatrist of Robert Enke, the German goalkeeper who committed suicide, and Enke's biographer Ronald Reng, who wrote *A Life Too Short*. I hope this programme will start as many conversations and discussions as the racism film did, and if it does I'll be absolutely delighted.

One of the ways I keep my head above water, given all of the things that are going on in my life, is by talking them through with the wonderful Mrs C. I don't know how she puts up with me sometimes, because occasionally there are just no answers to the problems I raise with her. The benefit to me of doing this is that I don't go stir crazy mulling things over. The benefit to Gem is that I get everything off my chest without acting out by going on a bender as I used to.

Last night I woke Gem up when I came to bed and told her that I feel like I'm going to explode very soon. I've got so much on that I feel like I'm spinning plates. I'm writing this book, filming the documentary, fulfilling my PFA duties, training and playing football, and all the while I am trying to be a good father and husband. As ever, Gem was incredibly calm and talked it through with me. The fact of the matter is that I can't cut down on any of my commitments. All of the things that I'm doing are necessary because they pay the bills.

As we talked it through, it became clear that I'm just going to have to box it all off into a finite time frame. The season is six weeks away from finishing and, once that is over, it will give me a lot more free time. The book needs to be written by the end of May and the documentary will be finished by the end of July. If I can focus on each of these deadlines, the workload will then drop off accordingly. Therefore, I've got to deal with six weeks of utter mayhem before it will all start to calm down. Once we looked at it that way, I saw that I would be able to handle that, and everything suddenly became less daunting. With that, I set the alarm for 5.30 and tried to get some sleep so I could be ready to start juggling all over again in the morning.

One of the great things about being a 'senior' member of the squad is that you can pontificate about 'the good old days'.

However, it can be quite embarrassing at times when I refer to 'Batfink' or 'Grotbags' and find that 90 per cent of the squad haven't got a clue what I'm talking about. I was utterly gobsmacked this week when one of the lads didn't know who the Spice Girls are. Really? Surely they're not that long ago. It was only then I realised that three of the lads in our first team squad are just three years older than my daughter. Oh my God, I am a senior citizen!

My saving grace is that I am not the oldest in the squad. Clive Platt has got a year or two on me, which therefore makes him my partner in crime when it comes to 'educating' the young lads. We are a modern-day Statler and Waldorf, though we will definitely be the only two who know who they are. We wax lyrical about original jungle music, old-school TV such as *Airwolf* and *Knight Rider*, and can remember the time when Gary Lineker actually played the game, though Alan Hansen and Mark Lawrenson are before even our time.

Every year the players vote for who they think are the best players they have come up against in their division that season. The votes are collated and the top 11 go into the PFA Divisional Team of the Year, announced at the PFA Awards dinner in London. The ballot papers have just been sent to our place and we all filled them out with a great deal of discussion. The most common question was: 'Who've you got at left-back? I can't think of one.'

This seems to be what happens most years, if I'm honest. There are some positions that just don't stand out, full-backs being one of them. I'd like to add centre-halves to that list but I know it's not true, and I'm only saying it because I've never been in a team of the season. I hadn't thought about that until now, and suddenly I realised that I would really quite like to have that honour on my CV. It was obviously still on my mind when the next game, against Oxford on 23 March, came around. We had barely kicked off when I called over to their striker, John Constable, when there was a break in play: 'Hey, big man. Did you vote for me in the team of the year?'

'You what?'

'Did you vote for me, for the PFA awards?'

'I can't say that I did, fella.'

'You've had a nightmare then, I'm gonna batter you today!'

He laughed, but I think I meant it; I went on to dominate him. Maybe that's what I need to get me in the zone: check if my opponent thinks I'm any good. If they don't, it's just another chance to prove someone wrong. What a pity I didn't work out this technique of self-motivation a little earlier in my career – who knows what I might have achieved?

CHAPTER 22

TWO-WEEK WONDERS AND THE NANDO'S CREW

We have come into some unbelievable form of late and at a very good stage of the season. Our home form is outstanding: we have won ten home games on the spin and are now sitting pretty in third place in the table, the last automatic promotion spot. The gaffer is trying to instil a belief in us that we can win the league. I think everyone wants to believe. We are 11 points off Gillingham at the top but we have a game in hand. I think we would have a greater belief if we could just win a bloody away match.

For some unknown reason, we cannot win an away game for love nor money. I have played in sides that can't win away and you can usually identify a reason. At Burnley in the Premier League, we had an awful away record. Home fixtures gave us the advantage of playing in a comparatively ramshackle stadium in the back of beyond – it wasn't the sort of set-up the Prem boys were used to. Furthermore, our fans were incredibly loud and intimidating and genuinely got us through games. Away from home we might as well have been playing at the Colisseum. The double blow for us was that the home team were in their comfort zone and generally performed far better there than at Turf Moor, but also a lot of our players were a tad overawed by playing in such huge stadiums against some big stars, lowering our own potency as a team. These two things combined meant that the gap between us was huge, and players of that calibre destroy you when they have an advantage.

Those reasons couldn't apply here, though. Sixfields is a tidy stadium, not overwhelming, not falling to bits, just tidy and well suited to League 2. The opposition weren't superstars either, so there was no reason for us to be found wanting at any of their grounds. It isn't even as though we are playing terribly away from home. The performances have actually been decent. We have been punished for any error that is made and then, instead of shutting up shop, we go hunting for the equaliser and try to make a game of it. This approach means we rarely lose 1-0. We either win or lose 3-1 because of our attacking strategy if we ever go behind. This may be something we have to address. We have two back-to-back away games coming up, and if we can get four or six points from them then I think we can guarantee automatic promotion, for only the second time in my career, which would be lovely.

I want to call us a bunch of shithouses, but I can't. Football is the weirdest game on earth. The away matches at Cheltenham and Bradford, two of our rivals in the promotion chase, both resulted in a 1-0 loss, even though we probably produced two of our best away performances of the season. It is quite infuriating how this happens. We created a host of chances in both games but just couldn't convert them. Then, to add insult to injury, the two goals we conceded came from a set piece against Cheltenham, usually our forte, and then a comical error between one of our defenders and our goalkeeper that cost us the game against Bradford.

I can't criticise our keeper, young Lee Nicholls, as he has been utterly outstanding for us all season. He's on loan to us from Wigan and it was a shock to me when I heard that he is just 19 years old. His head is physically massive, far too big for someone so young, so I'll have to check his passport one day. He has made saves that I have just had to applaud, there and then; he will have a very long career ahead of him, especially if he learns to use his voice, the only piece missing from the jigsaw.

Fortunately, we weren't made to pay the full price of these defeats, because all of the teams around us are faltering too. After ten consecutive home wins, we have a home match against my old employers York City, which could cement us in the automatic promotion spots and, by some cruel twist of fate, consign them to the bottom of the division and a swift return back to the Football Conference.

I draw no delight from the predicament that York find themselves in. I am actually completely gobsmacked that they have ended up where they are. It was a very tough decision to leave them from a professional angle; I genuinely believed that both sides would be in the promotion mix come the end of the season. For some reason, York went on a horrendous run of form after I left, resulting in Gary Mills being relieved of his duties, which surprised me. The impression I got from his chairman was that his only remit was to retain the club's league status, and I figured they would do that comfortably. His exit saw the return to league management of a man to whom I will forever be indebted, Nigel Worthington. He gave me my league debut at Blackpool back in 1997 and also my first professional contract, so he obviously knows a player when he sees one.

It's amazing how a change in management can radically alter the prowess of a squad, often with exactly the same group of players. I have seen several managers leave football clubs – many would say I've been the cause of a few departures – and have seen a variety of outcomes at the event. The two polar opposites in the context of impact both came at Burnley.

When Owen Coyle took over from Steve Cotterill, there was a palpable shift in the atmosphere around the club. Cotts had been at Burnley for many years and I think he had taken the squad as far as he could. His forthright and often tough manner had instilled a level of fear around the place. Owen came in and completely shifted the dynamic. His focus was on total enjoyment. It was fun at training, something that a lot of the squad hadn't encountered for a few years. This change led to a happy workforce, and a happy workforce is a productive one, as any businessperson worth their salt will tell you. This joy-infused team that was high on confidence went on to be incredibly successful, considering the players it contained. We were definitely a classic example of a team whose total was greater than the sum of its parts.

When Owen left the club we experienced the other end of the spectrum. We were in a run of bad form in the Premier League, but still in 13th place. The new boss needed to be dynamic, charismatic and someone who could make an immediate impact. After a couple of weeks, it was plain to see that Brian Laws didn't have those traits. The lads asked a few questions among ourselves when he was appointed, because he had recently left Sheffield Wednesday after taking them to the bottom of the Championship. We believed that the club was in a position to attract one of the bigger names in management, but obviously not. Had we done so, we might have drawn confidence from that, rather than wondering if he was the right man.

I genuinely believe we would have remained in the Premier League had Owen stayed, but we'll never know. Whatever the long-term impact of a new manager, you almost always find a short-term change in training levels and performance from the squad. We are desperate to impress the new boss. If you have been out of the frame, it is your chance to shine; if you have been playing every week, then you have to prove yourself all over again.

It is this period that used to rile my roomie, Graham Alexander, beyond the point of distraction. It infuriated him that we'd get the two-week wonders training well, who would then plummet back to their usual inept levels of performance once things calmed down. I love Grezza. He is the finest man I have met in football, and he's a very sociable guy. Seriously, he is the most professional man I've ever met and the finest example to any young person who wants a long career in football.

While York must have been hoping that they would benefit from the two-week wonders, because they are hovering perilously close to the edge, we were incredibly confident going into the game. I was named as captain, because Langers had picked up a knee injury that will keep him out for the remainder of the season. It's quite a significant blow to our chances, but not insurmountable.

Having seen how the York captain Chris Smith is incredibly superstitious while I was with him at the club, I tried to mess up his routine as much as possible. He has to be last out of the dressing room to meet the referee before the match; he has to wait for the opposition to be ready in the tunnel before he'll leave the dressing room; and he has to be last into the centre circle when the referee calls us for the toss before kick-off. I know that there are other things he does while he's getting ready, but I can't really affect those.

The best chance I had of playing with his mind was in the centre circle. When the ref called us in for the formalities, I hid behind one of our players near the centre circle. I could see Smudge hovering, walking up to and then away from the centre circle because he just had to be last in. The sponsors and mascots had all gathered there and he walked all the way up to the group, then spotted me and skipped away with a wry smile on his face. I burst out laughing and strolled into the middle, hoping I'd done enough to disrupt his thoughts.

I am all for routine, as it is a way of getting your mind prepared for the challenge that lies ahead. Repetition gets something 'in the bone', makes it a subconscious action or reaction, which is incredibly important when you are trying to reach your optimum performance state. Superstition, however, can be incredibly destructive. When you have a sequence of actions that you psychologically rely on to define the quality of your performance, even though there is no physical link between them, then you have lost a huge element of control over what you do. In other words, it makes perfect sense to do some stretching exercises before every game, but there is no benefit to be had from insisting that you have to put on your left sock first. The negative effect of not being able to fulfil one superstitious act far outweighs the positive effect of doing ten superstitious things right. Sadly, my Derren Brown mind games backfired in a very big way. Not only did York beat us 2-0, but Smudge had an outstanding game. Bollocks.

It is really hard to make lasting friendships in football because you've barely got to know someone and then either one or the other of you leaves and suddenly you find that you're at the other end of the country. This last four months has definitely seen a new friendship blossom in my life that was brought about only by sheer circumstance.

Jake Robinson's lease on his car had expired and, due to the fact that his contract is up at the end of the season and therefore he has no guaranteed work, he has been unable to commit to a new one. So he'd taken to riding his bike into training from his flat in the town, or even walking if it was a clear day. I was usually arriving in Northampton around half an hour early for training, as I had to allow time for the inevitable morning crashes on the M1, so I started to pick him up and give him a lift in.

Jake had already made his mark on me with his brilliant sense of humour. He has a really dry wit and randomly interjects with comments that often go unnoticed because they are so arbitrary and usually ridiculously intelligent. Spending this time with him before and after training meant we got chatting about far more personal stuff than the usual training ground content, and we have struck up a really good relationship, one that would never have had the chance to build if we didn't have this time together in the car.

The only other time that we see each other socially is in the 'Nando's Crew' that congregates the night before every home game. There is a hard core of lads who go every week without fail: Robbo, Bayo, Lee Nicholls, Lewis Moult, Joe Widdowson, Ishmel Demontagnac and me. We meet at the same time and all order the same food, so much so that we actually get a 'Cobblers discount' of 20 per cent off our bill. We are grateful, but the fact that the Northampton Saints rugby boys get 50 per cent off their bill leaves us feeling a little under-appreciated. I bet they eat twice as much as we do as well.

Robbo is an unbelievably disciplined lad. He has a degree in Sports Science and Nutrition, which he is constantly supplementing by reading the latest journals and papers on advances in diet. He takes his breakfast into work with him and it usually consists of shredded steak and eggs with some kind of green superveg. It made me think this morning that this sport can be so very unfair. My breakfast usually consists of three Venti Americanos and three Marlboro Menthol. I eat a bar of Dairy Milk or a bag of giant chocolate buttons every night and my lunch is always gargantuan, especially with the new chef's cooking. How is it fair that I do all this and still retain seven per cent body fat, and I get picked every weekend? If commitment and self-discipline were the only requirements to play football, Robbo would be a full international.

We qualified for the play-offs today with a fantastic draw away at Port Vale, who themselves secured automatic promotion with their point. It is a memorable day because, not only did I get on the scoresheet, but I did it with a left-foot volley. My left foot is for standing on, and in its current condition it's not even very good at that. I was up for a set piece and the ball came arcing in. It deflected off one of their players and looped in front of me, three yards out at the back post. My personal commentary was in full flow: 'CARLISLE . . . Yeeeeeeeeeeeeeeeessssssss!'

As we saw at Aldershot, I am absolutely lethal from that distance. It was only when I watched the replay on Sky Sports News that I realised I still managed to hit the inside of the post – I nearly bloody missed! As a defender, I never really know what to do when I score because it is such an infrequent occurrence. Even if I've gone into the game with a plan to do one of those celebrations that have great meaning and sentimental value, if I do actually score I just lose all sense of control and get carried away in the moment.

I have never felt emotion even near to the first goal that I ever scored, for Blackpool against Carlisle United. It was my home debut for the Seasiders. I was 17 years of age and my mum and dad were in the stands to witness their boy make his dream come true, and they were sitting alongside my grand-dad. It was 1-1 in the 90th minute and we got a corner. I knew they were in the stand behind the goal we were attacking. I strode my gangly frame up with the big men to get in the mix.

The ball was whipped in and flicked on at the front post by the dreadlocked head of Andy Preece. I had looped around to the back post and was closing in on goal. I had already made up my mind that I was going to head it, which meant I was leaning too far forward to change my mind, my balance wouldn't allow it. The ball was dropping lower and lower and my only chance to make a good connection was to dive. I launched myself at the ball and managed to make a clean connection. I opened my eyes (yes, they were closed) to see the ball nestling in the bottom corner – I had done it, I had scored the winner! I wheeled away towards my family with pure joy exploding out of every fibre of my being, pointing up towards them and unleashing an almighty bellow that was the unmistakable sound of unadulterated ecstasy. I have the sequence of photos from the next few seconds and you can see every muscle and sinew in my body is at maximum capacity.

Each goal I've scored since then has still been an incredibly exhilarating moment, but none of them has ever eclipsed the first. Today, I managed to regain my composure as all of the guys jumped on my back like some playground 'pile-on', and I pushed them away so that I could gesture to the crowd. The action was something I'd seen done by the Asian guy in the movie *Hangover*, when he was dumping the main characters in the middle of the desert.

'So long!' I shouted as I showed my open palm to the crowd. It took me all of three seconds to shut my mouth and trot back to the halfway line. We were at Vale Park and they had a capacity crowd expecting to seal promotion. My second-minute goal was not what they came for and they did not look pleased about it. I can't be inciting a riot now, can I? PFA chairman and all that, anyone would think that I would have some sense of responsibility. The final whistle brought about a result that kept everyone happy; even though it was an 85th-minute own goal that deprived us of all three points, at least it meant we weren't getting lynched in Wedgwood country.

CHAPTER 23

D FOR DISASTER

The PFA Awards dinner is our showpiece event of the year as a union. Every professional player across all four divisions votes for the footballer who they deem to have been the best performer for that season. We all converge on Park Lane in London for a black-tie dinner where we celebrate the successes of the season. It is even more significant for me because, as chairman of the union, this is where I give my big speech. I have to welcome and address the guests with a 15-minute speech in which I note all the major achievements throughout that year. I also take the opportunity to make any kind of moral or ethical points that have been brought to the fore by events that may have occurred.

This year was a chance to focus on many positives. We have had all of the various incidents involving racism and discrimination; but we have also seen many changes in the industry and the union itself that bode well for making progress in this area. It was also a momentous occasion for another and long overdue reason. For the first time in our history, we were joined by our female colleagues and we presented the inaugural Women's Player of the Year award.

It was a fantastic chance to celebrate the coming together of the sexes in an industry where there have been huge problems concerning the role of women. This was our night to show that football as an industry is willing to change, is open to change and leading by example.

Instead, it turned into an unmitigated disaster. I cannot catch my breath at the debacle that unfolded last night. It was without doubt the worst awards ceremony that I have been to as a professional, and the most embarrassing one that I have had the misfortune to chair.

The timings of the event were horrendous for a start. It is invariably a long night as it is, with a lot of hobnobbing, so we're usually quite *laissez faire* about everything running according to the schedule. However, we had an extra award to fit in tonight, so we knew that accuracy and brevity were going to be important. No such luck, as everything dragged way over time and we were looking at a post-midnight finish for an event that was due to wrap up at 11pm.

But however irritating that was, it was just a minor inconvenience. What happened on stage was something that will stain the reputation of the PFA for a long time, possibly forever. Our 'entertainment' for the evening was in the form of a comedian. We have for many years struggled to find someone who fits the bill in this regard. So many outstanding comedians have died a death on the stage at this do. Often they seem to believe that they are performing to a bunch of lewd and rowdy footballers, when the reality is that this is a corporate event. It's actually more than that, it is the most diverse audience that you could possibly imagine. As well as the players, we also have in attendance the football hierarchy, current and former legends, campaigners and inspirational heroes such as Doreen Lawrence, Kick It Out, Show Racism the Red Card, our newly joined peers from the women's game, and many, many more. Because of that, it is a veritable minefield when you want to be comedic or facetious about something. This is why we do brief them before they come on.

Imagine my horror, then, when the comedian's opening line was: 'Luis Suarez? He a ni**er!' WHAT? Did he just say that? I broke into an instant sweat. He continued in this vein for about ten minutes. 'Ni**er this, ni**er that,' I cannot tell you how much I was squirming in my seat. After all we have been through as an industry, this was just flying in the face of everything that we purport to stand for.

The guy could see that he was struggling; he soon realised that this wasn't the Comedy Store and his material was not hitting the target, so he changed tack: 'What about the Jews?' ARE YOU KIDDING ME? I sank lower into my chair and could barely look the man next to me in the eye. Yes, you guessed it, I was sitting next to the FA chief, David Bernstein.

This angle obviously paid no dividends, so the guy moves on to his next topic: having sex with white women. KILL ME NOW. I looked behind me and saw all of the journalists we had invited hovering around behind the top table. They looked as flabbergasted as I felt.

After the act had finished, I stepped into the group with sweat pouring down my face and a mouth drier than a Dubai drain. I had no explanation whatsoever. I didn't know what to say to these men. They wanted answers and understandably so, but I couldn't fly straight in without some kind of conflab with Gordon Taylor. I explained this to them and said I'd speak as soon as I possibly could, once I'd got any kind of acceptable reason for what had just happened.

Who in their right frame of mind books Reginald D. Hunter as the comedian of choice for this occasion? Don't get me wrong, this is what comedians do, and this is definitely what Mr Hunter does. When you go to a comedy club, you have to be prepared to leave your moral compass at the door. Comedians will push the boundaries of acceptability and take you to the edge of your comfort zone, oftentimes beyond that, and that is fine, I have no problem with that.

The difference here was that we had paid for this man to come and perform at our showpiece event of the year. Yet this repertoire completely undermined everything that we have done and fought for over the last 30 years, offending the majority of our guests on the night. What the hell were we thinking? A lot of people were caught unawares, because no one was expecting this sort of fallout. Nobody knew exactly how to respond. There was some shuffling around, some whispered conversations and some very red faces, but the matter wasn't actually addressed at the time. All I could do was assure the guys from the press that I would be available for comment the next day, but at the time it was a case of 'the show must go on'.

Returning to my seat I was compelled to apologise to Fabrice Muamba, who was our guest of honour, David Bernstein and chairman of the Football League Greg Clarke, the men in closest proximity. In reality I wanted to get up on the stage and apologise to everyone, to the world – it was a horrible situation. You might ask why I didn't. Well, this evening was supposed to be a night of celebration. My feeling was that we should let the attention return to its intended focus, the exploits of our finest players on the pitch, and the amalgamation of the men's and women's game. I felt we could deal with this situation in the morning so that the night wasn't a complete disaster.

The rest of the event went without any incident of note, but the damage had already been done, and it was critical damage. I retired to my room at around 1am with Mrs C, who I don't get to see over the course of the evening due to the layout and the formalities of the event. I already had eight missed calls and messages on my phone. The incident had happened barely two hours ago at a private event, but social media gets its incredibly long tentacles everywhere, and quickly. I was knackered at this point and just couldn't be bothered even to listen to the messages, as nothing would change over the next seven hours, and I felt I needed a good night's sleep.

When the sun rose on Monday morning, I was incredibly anxious as to what the papers would carry. Breakfast at the hotel was full of PFA employees absolutely flabbergasted at what had unfolded the night before. No one knew what to say or how to react, but we all knew that we had made a monumental mistake. My phone was like the bat phone – it did not stop flashing. I answered all the calls, but asked to be afforded a few hours so that the union could analyse what had happened and consider our response.

The press were very understanding about our position, but the football grapevine is electric. The meeting that I hoped to have never materialised either, as I couldn't get in touch with Gordon Taylor and nothing should go to press without his approval. The longer the day went on, the angrier and more embarrassed I became that we hadn't addressed this issue. Smiles and flippant comments are a response of the past; you can no longer maintain a wall of silence and just hope an issue goes away. We are usually the first to address incidents that arise, and quite right, too. If you mess up, you front up.

In the end, I decided I would have to step forward and say what I felt. So I did. I called one of the Sky Sports News anchors to see if they would be willing to send a crew around to my house so that I could address the situation myself. Bizarrely, they didn't really want to take up the story, but the guys at talkSPORT definitely did. I conducted an interview with them in the afternoon where I apologised unreservedly for what had occurred the night before. The crux of the matter was that, whether people were offended by the comedian's set or not, whether they found it humorous or not, it was wholly inappropriate for us to put that on show, and to put our invited guests in a position where they might be seriously offended. It felt good to face the issue, but I had to hope that I hadn't upset the apple cart by speaking in this way.

Gordon had been at a meeting all day, as football never sleeps. It emerged that Mr Hunter had been thoroughly briefed on the event and what was acceptable, but he put forward this routine anyway. He later claimed that we had lost our 'sense of irony' at the PFA, and it was even rumoured that we had asked him to repay his fee, but all we asked for was an apology as we had laid out what was required. Sometimes, you just can't legislate for the actions of an individual, but you still have to own your own part in the piece.

— CHAPTER 24 —

TUNNEL VISION

I am utterly delighted that Northampton have made the play-offs, and for more reasons than you might imagine. Obviously, there is the potential for success, something that every player wants every season, but very few actually achieve. Further to this, though, my journey is the sub-plot to the film I am presenting on depression and mental health issues. What a bonus it would be if we made it to Wembley. It's almost impossible to plan for a season ending like that, and it would just be perfect if we got there.

Even more than those reasons, I still need to finish this bloody book as well. I never realised how tough it would be to get almost 90,000 words down on paper. The play-offs have not only given me a bit of decent material to write about, but they've also afforded me a cheeky extension to the deadline and that is much needed. I frequently regret that I took on so many things at the same time: I must be a glutton for punishment; either that or clinically insane, and the jury is still out.

The feeling among the squad is one of focus and relative certainty, which is a very good balance without being too cocksure. In the weeks before this, we had been talking about the prospect of making the play-offs and the general consensus was that they are great, as long as you win. There is absolutely nothing to be gained from getting to the season-closing mini-tournament and not winning.

It actually creates a genuine paradox. Reaching the play-offs is always seen as the definition of a successful season. However, if you lose in the play-offs, at any stage, it sends the players, management and fans into the summer break with a feeling of utter failure. Where is the sense in that?

This makes even less sense when you consider the situation of Barnsley. If you had asked anyone associated with the club at the beginning of the season what would constitute a successful campaign, I can bet that most would have said they expected to achieve a top ten finish, despite the fact that they had been in the bottom half of the league for the previous few years. In actual fact, they survived relegation from the Championship on the last day of the last season by a solitary point, and then proceeded to celebrate like they'd won the bloody league. Their players were on Twitter thanking all and sundry and the club went on a trip to Vegas. How can a team that finishes 21st be left with better feelings than three of the teams that finish third, fourth, fifth or sixth? It is just not right.

With a couple of weeks to go in our season in League 2, we'd got wind that there were players from other teams who had a chance of finishing in the play-offs who were adamant they didn't want to. One lad said he hated his gaffer and couldn't stand the thought of him getting any praise for the team being successful, as he thinks he's a clown. Unbeknown to the manager concerned, he had the last laugh because the team went up automatically. Another squad had several players who had already booked their holidays for the first week in May, which was incredibly pessimistic. Ultimately, I think most players would say that if we don't win, the play-offs are not worth it, and I must admit that those are definitely my thoughts. But to avoid that, for these three weeks I have one focus: I am going to Wembley and I am going to get me a medal. It will probably be the last medal of my career, but it would definitely be the most satisfying.

It must be the end of the season. The drugs testers have ventured beyond the M25 and come to visit us at Northampton. This is the first year in a long time that I've not been tested at all. I used to have a bit of paranoia about it, if I'm honest. I am aware that 'target testing' is a tactic used when players are considered in the high-risk category, and I just assumed that someone figured I had to be on something.

The test itself is just downright degrading. You are assigned an invigilator who cannot leave your side until you have filled, sealed and packaged your pee. On a training day it's not so bad. You are usually fairly hydrated and can fill the bottle with relative ease. On a match day it is a completely different proposition. It can take some lads hours to fill the bottle to the required line. You end up sitting in a room with half a dozen grumpy old men (I'm sure they don't really want to be there either) while you ply yourself with litre after litre of water. I have known several clubs just leave players behind because they can't pee. You can't even have a shower or anything, just in case you accidentally wee.

Once the notice has been served that you have been chosen for testing, it is your very next production of urine that needs to be tested. When you finally feel like you can go, you are tailed by this guy to the toilet who watches you as you wee in a bottle. I don't mean from outside the cubicle either; he literally has to sit eye level with your penis and watch the fluid flow into the bottle. It's humiliating, especially if you suffer from piss fear. Some lads just freeze because someone's watching. After that you have to decant your own piss into two other bottles which are then sealed and packed away, but it isn't totally over. They have to test a little bit in front of you to see if it's dense enough. If you are too hydrated it doesn't count! What a ridiculous system where you almost drown yourself in water to force a piss out, and then they tell you it's not good enough and you have to wait until you're more dehydrated.

The kicker is that when you have finally produced your first wee, you then can't stop pissing for the next four hours, especially if you've got a hamster bladder like mine. I've never known a player who has failed a drugs test, although I have heard second- and third-hand stories about them. You're never sure what to believe in football, but there's usually no smoke without fire, or at least some very hot coals. There is a story about one manager at a club I once played for who used to shout to his squad at the training ground: 'The drugs guys are here. If any of you have been up to no good, get over the back.' At which point some players would hotfoot it over the back fence and through the trees while the boss made some excuse for their non-attendance. I don't know how true it is, but I bet it's not that far away and I bet that something like that happened at more than one club. Fortunately, there have been no such dramas in my career.

I love how meticulous Aidy is. Our training for the play-off semi-finals against Cheltenham has been rigorous and high intensity. I would have expected no less. The psychological preparation has just been taken to a whole new level, though. We had the standard meetings about tactics, form, set pieces, with various other bits of video about what Cheltenham do, but then we did something that I have never done before: we practised lining up in the tunnel. Yes, we trained at how to walk out of the dressing room, wait alongside our opponents and enter the field of play.

I have played at many clubs where even the suggestion of such a thing would have caused laughter, dismay and a certain level of incredulity, but it says so much about this group of players and what Aidy has cultivated that we set about it as though it is something we do every week. After all, many people remember that famous moment when Roy Keane squared up to Patrick Vieira in the tunnel before an Arsenal v United game, and how significant it was deemed to be.

The result of our practice session turned out to be incredibly interesting and brought us to a conclusion that we didn't expect. The gaffer split the squad into two teams and put us in separate dressing rooms at the stadium. We chatted in our groups about what would make the biggest impact in that short space and time between opening the dressing-room door and going on to the pitch, and we came to very similar conclusions. Our group wanted to be big and loud, with lots of aggressive shouts to indicate that we were focused and up for it. This may seem a little contrived, and it can be if the player doesn't have the natural demeanour or physique to carry it off.

I will never forget the impact that Danny Shittu had on opponents before games when I played for Queens Park Rangers. He would bound out of the dressing room with no shirt on, 19 stones of prime beef, letting out monosyllabic Neanderthal grunts and screams, flexing his muscles and beating his chest all the while. Some players turned their noses up at this blatant display of machismo, but a lot of players were open-mouthed at what was before them, clearly intimidated by his sheer size and overflowing levels of testosterone.

We also decided to make the other team wait for us in the tunnel, prolonging that period of nervous energy that all players experience before the game. The only drawback was that the other group had the same idea. We popped our heads around the dressing-room door to see them sneaking a peak into the corridor too, and both doors slammed shut like some naughty kids trying to sneak downstairs in the middle of the night. A Mexican stand-off ensued, neither group willing to concede, until we revised our strategy.

How do you counter strategic delays? With cold, hard, unperturbed focus. So we decided to get out there first and line up like a military machine, forward facing, chests puffed out, not interacting or responding to anything that came through the other door, and it was good. As we analysed it afterwards, the lads in the other group said how disconcerting it was to see everyone lined up, ready, focused and unflinching, so we adopted this as our game plan. Aidy added one or two little extras too, which included standing slightly in front of the opponent alongside you, and also standing uncomfortably close to them, invading their personal space. This really was getting into the minutiae of the battle; I could see Sun Tzu smiling from his war room in the sky.

The first leg of the semi-final went as close to the plan as possible. We were awesome in the tunnel, like a military unit. We then took that on to the field and gave Cheltenham an absolute pasting. We could have scored three or four, but had to settle for a delicate 1-0 win. Considering we hadn't beat Cheltenham during the main season, this was an excellent start. It also placed the onus on them to attack us in the second leg. I know our away form is patchy, but our counter-attacking qualities are second to none.

This was only stage one completed in a three-stage event. The squad was very calm in the dressing room afterwards, which was good to see. Because we haven't got that many players who have been through this before, I thought we might have to pull one or two down from the ceiling, but instead the calm, confident focus remained. This really could be it.

We finished the job at Whaddon Road with a resolute performance and an absolute wonder strike from Luke Guttridge, a 30-yard volley that nestled under the crossbar. Add to that the fact that we actually won a game away from home for once and it was the consummate performance. Young Nathan Cameron alongside me was colossal. I didn't feel like I had my best game, but we kept a clean sheet and that's my job done. Once more, there weren't any over-exuberant celebrations. We came off the pitch like we had done two-thirds of the job, and the rest was yet to come.

When we got back on the bus, the atmosphere shifted again. Alex Nicholls had been coming to the games for the past month. He is so desperate to get back in the frame that he hobbles along with us, lugging this huge contraption of a leg brace with him, and supports us from the bench. I'm sure the only reason he comes is to play Monopoly at the back of the bus. Yes, I said Monopoly. Gone are the days of the high-rolling poker table or the ridiculous three-card brag (a game that should never be played by competitive men with a lot of money). I have to admit that I am a little bit disappointed that my Mario Kart school has been depleted, but all alternatives have been replaced by Monopoly on Tozer's iPad, and he wasn't even allowed to play as he gets so angry it can upset his concentration in the game.

The iPad wasn't out tonight, though. The lads were tucking into some pizzas and there were a few bottles of lager floating around. At the back of the bus, the whole situation was sinking in for Nicho. He had had the worst season of his life: injured since October and repeatedly suffering setbacks over the duration, he was now about to miss out on a Wembley final. He had used up all of his resolution just to be at the games, and so this was now a hefty blow. He was incredibly emotional on the bus and the boys took it in turns to try to reassure him.

I moved over to him when he wasn't talking to anyone and tried to find the right words to say. What do you tell a guy who has missed more than half a season? What do you say when you know he is going to miss out on what would have been his first ever trip to Wembley? Nothing, that's what. I knew that there was nothing I could possibly say that would make him feel any better in this situation, so I just kissed him on the top of the head and gave him a hug.

The next day I called Bayo on the phone. He has his own clothing range, the Beast Mode brand. I asked him if he would be able to get a full set of Beast Mode t-shirts made with Nicholls on the back. He instantly loved the idea. I don't want to be presumptuous about the outcome of the game, but I do want Nicho to know that as a squad we are thinking about him. What a great gesture it would be to climb the steps wearing shirts that honour him. There are so many reasons to win this game I just can't even contemplate us losing. It almost feels like it's our destiny. Let's try to inject a bit of sunlight into this man's season.

Before we got into the Wembley preparations, I had a day that I've been looking forward to for months: a round of golf. This wasn't just any round of golf, though; it was Brian Jensen's Testimonial Golf Day and a chance to catch up with my old compadres once more. I hadn't played for over a year and so I was expectedly terrible, but as any golf enthusiast will know, it takes only one good shot to keep you coming back.

It was a really enjoyable day and I was glad I could at last contribute to Beasty's season of events; I had missed a couple of earlier ones. Beasty has been a brilliant servant to Burnley. He has seen off more rivals for his number one shirt than I have had clubs. I have never known a player to have so many guys brought in to replace him, only to step up his game another notch and banish them to the bench. I admire that a lot. He is also the only person I know who has a sausage named after him!

Another of my former team-mates missed out on the event, but under altogether different circumstances. He appears to be on the edge of oblivion. I can see his actions and understand his mindset, and I know exactly where it is leading. One good thing about having been through all that I have is that I am aware of similarities in other people's lives. This then gives me an opportunity to reach out and hopefully prevent them from going where I've been. The flipside to that is that some people just don't want to hear what you have to say, even though all of the evidence is slapping them in the face and has been doing so for years. I have got to the point with this individual where I just have to accept that he is not ready. All I can do is continually keep my door open for him, as and when he realises that he needs it. It's a shame because he is a fantastic guy, but his actions have resulted in him losing many good friends and this will continue to happen until he shakes off his denial. I hope it won't be long before he realises the situation he's in, and when he does I'll be ready to help.

CHAPTER 25

WHAT DEFINES ME

A Wembley final is such a one-off occasion that it is incredibly hard to know how to prepare for it. Chris Hackett, Kelvin Langmead and I have all played there before, so we have some sort of insight into what it will be like. The rest of the squad are about to embark on a journey into the unknown, and that poses a significant problem for the manager. Football is such an imperfect science that the best a manager can hope for is to eliminate as many of the unknowns as possible by preparing the team with as much physical and mental information as possible.

It's for this reason that we are taking a trip to Wembley for a tour of the stadium in an attempt to take the 'wow' factor away from the players before the day. We travelled down en masse and had a look around the dressing room and stood on the hallowed turf. I know I'm not Rio Ferdinand and haven't played here 40 times, but I defy any player not to be slightly overwhelmed by the place and all that Wembley stands for. It is an institution, it is the home of football, and it is magnificent.

I stood at the back of the group and tried to maintain

some kind of dignified silence, but inside I was screaming: 'THIS IS WHAT I'M TALKING ABOUT!' I cannot express to you how big an occasion this is. I'm 33 years of age, my body is virtually decrepit from the toll of 17 years of joints pounding and clunking, of heading tens of thousands of footballs, of being emotionally tossed this way and that, and it all brings me to here: I'm about to play at Wembley. I'm just a kid from Preston, from the humblest of beginnings and with moderate ability, who had a dream in his head and a fire in his belly. I've managed to get *back* to Wembley and show that it wasn't a fluke. I cannot wait for this.

Bringing myself back to the present, I try to remind the boys that getting to Wembley isn't the goal, winning at Wembley is. Soak it up, savour every moment of it all because it doesn't happen every year, especially not for players in League 2, but remember that we are here to do a job and that is what we have to focus on.

Bradford have the added advantage of having played here earlier in the season. They defied all odds to make it to the League Cup final against Swansea, a remarkable achievement. The reality is that they got battered 5-0 and their memories of the place will not be entirely positive. If we can start with a high tempo and put them under pressure, maybe get an early goal, it is entirely plausible that they will regress to a similar state of mind as they had back in March. As human beings we are creatures of habit and, when we are thrown into a set of circumstances, we revert to our most common and recent point of reference. Being under the cosh and a goal down at Wembley in front of 60,000 people will not take Bradford to a happy place; we need to seize that opportunity.

Our training has been adjusted this week to try to get us to acclimatise to the 1.30 kick-off time that the final is scheduled for. Aidy has made us report at nine for breakfast, rest for the remainder of the morning, eat lunch together and then train at what will be game time come Saturday. It's yet another piece of minute, detailed planning that we come to expect from the boss.

It has left us with two whole mornings to fill, but we have to be in complete rest at the same time. What better to do than go to the flicks? Thursday and Friday morning we walked up to the cinema at Sixfields and had special screenings put on just for us. We watched *Iron Man 3* on the Thursday and then *Fast and Furious 6* on Friday. I cannot catch my breath that there has been enough interest in these films for them to make six of the bloody things.

I can just about get my head around *Iron Man*. He's a superhero with superpowers: of course he can fly and defy the laws of physics in order to save the day, and Robert Downey Jr is ridiculously cool as Tony Stark – men want to be him, women want to be on him. On the other hand, Vin Diesel, the Rock and their mates are supposed to be normal people. How on earth can they jump off the roof of a car at 160mph, fly through the air and catch a woman who's fallen from a helicopter and then land comfortably, spooning on the bonnet of another car? It is utterly ludicrous. And as for the closing scene, they must have used the M1 as the runway; it went on for about 300 miles. But say what you like about the Hollywood ending, it may be predictable but it does leave you with the feel-good factor, the inescapable belief that good will prevail and all will live happily ever after. I fancy being Dwayne Johnson this weekend!

Wembley is the perfect setting for me to take a stroll off into the sunset, trophy in hand, whistling as I walk. What a glorious way to end my career this could be and I just can't help thinking that this is how it was meant to be. I nearly fell out of the game at the end of last season, but it just wasn't my time. This is my time; this is exactly how I envisaged the story to play out – captain, at Wembley for one last triumphant hurrah. Step aside Mr Downey Jr, because tonight I am going to be *Iron Man 4*.

I encountered a very strange notion last night. It's the night before the biggest game of the season and I was sitting on my hotel bed in Sopwell House, St Albans. The night before, I had stayed up really late, until about midnight, as I usually do two nights before a game. My logic is that if I'm up late on the Thursday, I'll sleep like a baby on the Friday – and I don't mean waking up every four hours for some milk. I lay in bed last night, having the standard daydreams about scoring a Wembley hat-trick, when a question popped into my head.

'What if you stayed up all night?'

But why would I do that?

'Then, if you had a stinker tomorrow, you would have a reasonable excuse, at least for you.'

I laughed out loud at my own crazy mindset. I can't believe that the thought of self-sabotage crossed my mind, just to give me an internal escape route from the responsibility for my performance the next day. I wonder if other lads get similar thoughts to these. When I think back on my life, I'm sure this has been a method for validating a lot of my behaviours. I don't know if I'm over-analysing it, but it would make sense in certain cases. I never used to go to casinos unless I got drunk. I think in some warped way I was consciously ridding myself of the ability to make coherent decisions, knowing that my urge to gamble would be sated with little contest. I vaguely remember starting arguments with the missus in order to have an excuse to storm out of the house and go to the pub. This would be a similar thing: creating the reason that justifies the subsequent action. Maybe I'll need a few more therapy sessions; I've just opened a whole new can of worms.

I don't think there is a day in the life of a footballer that can rival that of a Wembley final. I slept well after all, and when I awoke it was with that instant boundless energy with which I used to greet Christmas morning. What an awesome day this could be. I have purposefully tried to play it down up until now, but I just can't get away from the feeling that this is a huge day for me. After being tossed around from pillar to post over the past two years, this could be the day that I bring some vindication to my continued involvement in the game.

I tried to retire at the end of last season but it just didn't happen. I came crawling back to the game, cap in hand, and went on *Soccer AM* to beg for a club. My pride was in pieces. I felt like I had come to the point where I needed football but football didn't need me. If ever there was a situation that questioned your validity as a person, this was it, for a footballer at least. I was incredibly lucky that Gary Mills gave me an opportunity to get back into the game.

Now, nine months later, I had woken up with the chance to bring this situation around full circle. Not only had I managed to get back in the game, but I had contributed to a team that was on the brink of success and I was about to lead them out, as captain, at Wembley, the home of football. This has got to be one of the greatest mornings of my professional life. I know exactly what this means to me, I know exactly how valuable this day is, and I am going to milk it for all it's worth.

My ankle has restricted my ability to train fully all week, but there's no chance of it stopping me from playing today. I have already prepped the physio. I need an anaesthetic ready in case the painkillers aren't enough to take the pain away. I will be playing this game and no shitty little piece of floating bone is going to stop me. I've ironed my shirt, polished my shoes and even had a bath. I almost never have a bath, but today is special.

I can already see it in my mind's eye: walking up the steps at the end of the game, the same steps I walked up four years ago with Burnley. If we win today, I am 99 per cent certain that I will retire. My body has barely coped with the rigours of League 2 this year, and there is absolutely no way that it would be able to withstand League 1. If we don't win, then I think I will almost definitely play again next year. I can just see the shadow of unfinished business looming over my thoughts, constantly poking me in the shoulder about getting so near yet so far away from the prize, which could be a very tough one to shake off. I am so excited about it all that I am going to have to play some Words With Friends or something; I need to take my mind off it. I'm about to play my third play-off final, one in every division, and the prospect of promotion out of all three leagues in my career. What a beautiful day this could be.

I know that all of my family will be here today. They're all gathered to witness the glorious swansong of what has been a rather turbulent career. I always try to play down the fact that they are in attendance, but the truth is that it does make me want to put on a show. My aim today is to try to change my son's view of the game. I have told you how he doesn't like football. Daddy's 'work' is the reason that I am always battered and bruised, why I'm always away from home and am constantly missing things like his first nativity and birthday parties; he hates football. Even the persuasive powers of his mum are futile. Gem has spent the last couple of days getting out all of my football mementos, showing Marley photos and old shirts, trophies and medals, desperately trying to rouse a little bit of enthusiasm for this season finale. She even found his first-ever football shirt, a Burnley kit with 'Marley 5' on the back.

'How about we frame this shirt and hang it up in your bedroom, like Daddy has done with his shirts in his office?' she asked him in a desperate attempt to gain favour.

Marley pondered this for a moment and then replied, 'Or, why don't we frame a picture of me in my golf outfit with my golf clubs?'

I hate thinking that anything is a lost cause, but trying to get my boy interested in football is as close to one as you can get.

When the final whistle blew it was a horrible moment. This was not how it was meant to go. Not for one minute had I contemplated the fact that we might lose. I had batted around the different possibilities with regard to my own performance, embarrassing myself, excelling myself and all in between, but actually losing the game just wasn't an option.

I stood on the halfway line and watched the polar opposites of football emotion. One half of the stadium was in raptures, utterly ecstatic at what was a convincing and comfortable victory. They were on the up, moving forward to a new league, new opponents and an elevation in professional life and professional reputation. The other half – my half, our half – were disconsolate in abject defeat.

It wasn't even close. There was never a point in the game to get excited about, from the moment the first goal went in on 12 minutes. The whole event was one huge anticlimax and, to make matters worse, I am less than 40 yards away from my family. I can barely lift my head to look them in the eye. My two youngest children are in tears, with my wife desperately trying to console them, to reassure them that it's all okay.

The hurt, shame, sorrow, embarrassment and despair in that moment is quite possibly the worst feeling in football. If I could have summoned a very localised collision of tectonic plates that caused a two by two-yard hole to open up under my feet and allowed the belly of the earth to consume me in blistering fires, I would have chosen that over the next hour's parade of shame.

There are several things you must do to maintain honourable conduct in defeat, but it takes every remaining ounce of strength and will in your body to actually perform them. Firstly, your conquerors must be faced, one by one, to shake their hands and congratulate them. I just want to scream at them, to react in some petulant and disrespectful way because they have taken from me the very thing I wanted, but I don't, we don't: 'Congratulations, fella. Well played. All the best next season.'

One of the hardest sentences in the world.

Then you have to face the crowd. Tens of thousands of people have made this pilgrimage to the home of football, at great cost and with greater expectations, all to be let down by me when it comes to the crunch, by us. The walk around the perimeter of the pitch is long and slow; somehow it's harder than the 90 minutes of torture that you've just endured. It's so difficult because there is no way to avoid the emotions of the moment. You can see them etched across the faces of each and every person you have the gall to look at in the eye. Some people are tearful, some are angry, some are already out of the doors and on their way home and the others, well, they just look shocked.

I can't look as I walk past my family. My parents, my siblings, my wife and children, I just wanted to show them all, one last time, that I have something special: the ability to transform the lives of a team, a club and its fans, all in the course of 90 minutes. Well I did, I showed them that I can piss on the chips of a whole town in one easy step. I trudged past them with my head low. I came to a halt at the halfway line and tried to absorb the scene in front of me.

Bradford – the opposition, the enemy – were prancing around in sheer ecstasy. Champagne was spraying all over; the cameras were hustling around them like a swarm of ants on the leftovers of a summer picnic. Flags were flying high and pre-made t-shirts were being donned to pay tribute to whoever had previously inspired. As I watched, I mellowed. I hurt, I really hurt, but I don't hate. I know I gave all I had and I can see that my team-mates did too. Today just wasn't our day.

It feels a little bit like you're a naughty puppy getting your nose rubbed in your own mess when you have to stand and watch your adversaries climb the Wembley steps and take their spoils. As I looked on, a really strange feeling came over me; I wanted to applaud. I wasn't sure if the boss would like that, and I was damn sure our fans would hate it, but I had to give this team their dues. They may have deprived me of my dream, of my happy and glorious ending, but they did it fairly, they did it with style, and they well deserved their plaudits. My hands started to come together in a slow and quite laboured applause, but applause nonetheless. I had to recognise that we were beaten by a better team today, and it made me feel a little bit sick. Where was my Hollywood ending? Where was my *Iron Man* closing scene where I finally hold a trophy aloft as the leader of reformed ragamuffins who became an elite football unit?

Aidy ushered us all inside while Bradford continued to parade their trophy. Sad, dejected and silent, we sat down in a dressing room that suddenly felt absolutely enormous. He called us to attention and gave us a man-by-man appraisal of our season. Last year Northampton were on the verge of dropping into the bleak world of non-league football, yet, in 12 short months, we had transformed ourselves into play-off finalists. He told us that we couldn't let this unmitigated success be clouded by the paradox of 'failure' in a season finale. We have grown, we have improved, and tonight we will celebrate this fact with a party back at Northampton.

I hadn't drunk alcohol for a long time, but there was an urge within me to get absolutely trollied. The crates of lager were in the dressing room and we all tucked in, each in our own world of regrets, replays and reconstructions of the day's events. Feeling a little bit like 'Frank the Tank', I got showered and changed as quickly as possible, desperate to get away from the scene of this heinous crime and closer to the prospect of a journey to oblivion.

The route to the coach was through a gauntlet of journalists. They were just doing their jobs, I know, but it felt like they drew sheer delight from making you relive every emotion of this torrid day. In these circumstances, the first interview you give is always the best. It's heartfelt, your words are genuine and your feelings raw. As you drift down to the sixth, seventh and eighth guy (there wasn't a woman in sight), it all becomes a re-enactment of the first one. It's mechanical, disingenuous and just a ball ache if I'm honest.

I just want to get on the bus and have another beer, and this guy who has never kicked a ball in anger in his life is asking me to explain why we 'choked', to dissect our preparation and give clear and reasonable judgements on 'why you failed'. FUCK OFF! The press can have a really unique way of making you feel like a piece of worthless shite without you having any way of completely honest recourse. Responses are careful, diplomatic and politically correct when, in reality, you just want to say: 'Yes, I feel like shit. I let my whole world down today and now I am going to consume both of our bodyweights combined in alcohol to try to forget, or at least suppress, the whirlwind of self-loathing, shame, anger, embarrassment and utter despair that I am feeling right now.'

After breaking for freedom through the big double doors that lead to the team bus, I thought I was in the clear and away from this nightmare, but there was one more slap in the face to come. I went to step on the coach when there it was, right in front of me, the big, shiny trophy all dressed in Bradford City's colours. I had to touch it. I stepped on to their bus and picked up the prize that had eluded me. I really, really, REALLY wanted to lift this trophy today – it was the only chance I have ever had to lift a trophy as captain. Fuck, now I am going to get drunk.

'Wrong bus, mate,' said their coach driver without a hint of malice.

I smiled, backed down the steps and strode off through the warren of tunnels underneath Wembley Stadium. I sat myself down next to a big stack of stinking wheelie bins and lit one of Marlboro's finest. This was not how it was meant to be.

The journey back to Northampton was quite a quick one, speeded up by the constant flow of lager. I was five bottles deep by the time we pulled up at the Hilton hotel and jumped off the coach ready for action. I swept my bags up from under the bus and turned around to head for the bar when I was pounced on by two beautiful little people.

'Daddy!' they screamed as they leapt into my arms. My two little babies showered me in kisses, as my two big babies watched from afar. Gem, Fran, Marley and Honey May were ready and waiting to deliver me from my pain.

'I hungry, Daddy. I need wee-wee,' announced Honey May, while Marley was smacking me around the head with the biggest flag I've ever seen.

'Look, Dad. I've got a scarf too, and I had a hot dog!' It was clear that Marley and Honey were unaffected by the events of the day. A couple of big hugs from Gem and Fran showed me that they weren't too upset either. I settled my family down to eat some food at the restaurant, because the party buffet wasn't due to be ready for a couple of hours and it was already seven o'clock, nearly the kids' bedtime never mind teatime. Mrs C looked at me with what seemed like concern on her face.

'We're not staying late are we?'

'No danger, my love. We're just going to stay a couple of hours and then get off to bed; it's been a long day.'

'Are you getting smashed?'

'Don't be silly. That's not on my agenda any more. I'm way past that, Gem.'

'You might be past it . . .'

And I understood her concerns. I had built this day up so much, lain huge significance on the outcome, and it had ended up being everything we didn't want. All of my past reactions at times like this had been exactly the same: drink and forget the world – why would it be any different this time? It would be different because I am different; because we are different. We have come through the full circle of play-off final emotion together, from Gem's first tentative steps in my life when we lost in Cardiff, to winning but not playing against Leeds, to the unparalleled joy against Sheffield United and now, finally, this. Her understanding of what the game means to me as a determined competitor, pride-seeking husband and providing father is total. What has fundamentally changed since 2003 is that we are now a loving family unit, and that supersedes anything that happens outside of our home.

We went into the party and relaxed in the company of family and friends. It wasn't the party we wanted, it wasn't the party I had planned, but it was nice. I danced with my kids in that 'embarrassing dad' way, and I loved it. The younger two started to sing songs about going home around ten o'clock, and so we made our way to our rooms. Bless them; they were so shattered that they were asleep as their heads hit the pillow. Fran, on the other hand, was having a serious issue with her friends. There were texts going back and forth that had brought her to tears. I am tolerant of many things in this world, but I will never accept anything that causes harm or distress to my kids. Gem, Fran and I sat in our pyjamas on a hotel bed, armed with pizzas, chocolate and fizzy pop, and sorted through the situation. As I cuddled Fran and her mascara-stained tears ran down her face and soaked my shirt, I realised that this is my Hollywood ending.

Ten years ago, almost to the day, I lost a football match in similar circumstances. That was the precursor to a period in my life when I virtually abandoned my family. I ran away from my daughter, I ignored my future wife-to-be for months and I hunted for the solution to my pain. I looked at the bottom of every bottle, glass and jar that I could find, and it almost led me to destruction.

Fast forward to now. I've lost a game that is probably slightly more important in the context of my career, as it is highly unlikely that I'll get here again. The difference this time is that it isn't the football match that defines me. Winning that game doesn't give me my value in life. Sitting at the end of a bed with my daughter in my arms, helping her through a situation that means more to her than any football match ever will, that defines me.

The kids are tucked up in bed and Mrs C is snuggled on 'her' side of our bed, even though we're in a hotel. I jumped into bed alongside her and rapped my head against the wooden headboard with an almighty clunk. Without even looking at me, my beautiful wife said: 'You've had a complete shitter today.'

And we laughed, uncontrollably, from the belly, until we could laugh no more.

We woke in the morning and the squad went their separate ways. Driving up the M1 with my family all snoozing in the car, I felt a huge sense of relief. It's over, for another year at least. Now we can look forward to a break. I'd love to sleep for a week, but that's just not going to be possible with these kids, and I wouldn't change it for the world. Hopefully we'll get a holiday abroad; if not, at least a bit of sunshine here in Blighty. Either way, I am going to switch off from football for a few weeks, spend some quality time with my family and get ready for whatever the next chapter brings.

A famous person once said, 'Life's a bitch, and then you die,' but I'm inclined to disagree. Life doesn't always give you what you want, but you will find true happiness when you appreciate having what you need.

EPILOGUE

Three days after Wembley, on 21 May 2013, I officially retired from football. Now, one month later, the magnitude of that decision is setting in. I sat down with Aidy in a post-season appraisal and told him exactly how I felt, both physically and mentally. I half-expected him to tell me that I was wrong, that he refused to accept my decision or something like that, but I should have known better. He was sitting at his desk with a pad and paper ready to minute our discussion. When I concluded my monologue, he just sat back in his chair and smiled at me, a knowing and accepting smile.

'I had a feeling that this was coming,' he said, looking straight at me – no, into me from his seat of power. 'Are you sure?'

'I'm one hundred per cent sure, boss. They say: "You know when you know," and I know; both my head and my body know.'

'Okay, son.'

He leant forward and scribbled two words on his pad, doubly underlined:

EPILOGUE

<u>Clarke – Retired</u>

And there it was in black and white, the end of my career.

'I thought you'd try and talk me out of it, boss. I thought you might not let me do it.'

'You know I'm all about choice, Clarke. This time it's different, I can see that. I knew you were making the wrong decision last year, I knew you would be back. This time, well, you're right. You just know!'

We spent some time reminiscing about wonderful moments and ridiculous moments from our five years together, never mind the rest of my life. It was on the verge of getting emotional; in fact, it got very emotional. We hugged. I left Sixfields as an ex-footballer, and it felt great; so great that I stopped at Burger King and had a bacon double cheeseburger with fries, supersize.

I wasn't sure how long that feeling would last; novelty generally wears off as realisation sets in. As each day passes, my happiness and contentedness deepen. There is a sense of relief that is liberating. So many feelings have been released from my life. The unrelenting consciousness of total recuperation, fitness and diet is no longer there. The stress about what club I'll play for, where they'll be and whether I need to move the family has gone. The dark cloud of expectation and responsibility that hangs over the modern-day footballer has completely dissipated. I am free!

So what now for this ex-pro? The documentary is in the edit suite and I am really looking forward to its transmission. This book is finally done and dusted, lifting another pressure from my mind. I had a meeting with Gordon Taylor, as my retirement means I will have to relinquish my role as chairman of the PFA. I have immensely enjoyed the role over the past three years, through all the trials and tribulations. It has given me an insight into the mechanics of football which I could never have understood without it. I have immersed myself into the work so much that I hope I can continue to contribute in some way moving forward, but handing over the role is constitutionally unavoidable.

I have dipped my toe into the world of corporate speaking with two events, one for Vodafone Global and one for Goldman Sachs. They were thoroughly enjoyable and hopefully I will be invited to do more. My desire, as I'm sure many will have guessed by now, is to go into media and broadcasting. I have finalised a contract with ITV that gives me the entry into the industry that I have worked for. I have the excitement and anticipation in my stomach that I remember from 1997; the desire to learn, work hard and prove myself in this difficult new world. It's awesome.

The greatest conclusion to all of this for me is that I can now give Gem the opportunity to focus on what she wants to do in life, to work towards what she wants to achieve. It's not as selfless as it sounds. This is what relationships should be. I've been the centre of our world for ten years now; where's the give and take in that? Now is the time for me to support her. I was always so scared of what would fill the huge void left by football when the answer was right under my nose. There's a golf lesson at 2pm today. It has been the source of excitement for the past four weeks now. Marley will finally get to show me what he has learnt while daddy was at 'work'.

ACKNOWLEDGEMENTS

Firstly, thank you to my editor, Ian Marshall. You took one never-ending paragraph and moulded it into something that resembles a book.

Thank you to Racheal Smith and your mum and dad, Pat and John. You saved my life and I am forever indebted to you x

Thank you to Melissa Chappell – your guidance and support have opened my world to a growing number of opportunities.

Thank you to Peter Kay, you are my Yoda. I would never have developed the tools I need to progress without you. I love you, Chef.

Thank you to Aidy Boothroyd and Keith Mincher, the biggest influences in my professional life. You make each day an 'embarrassingly well' one.

Thank you to Mum, Dad, Marvin, Bianca and Anni. A family unit built on love and respect that I will forever treasure.

Thank you to my beautiful children, Francesca, Marley and Honey May. You are the greatest things that I have ever 'done' in my life. I love you all xx

Finally, and in every way the most important acknowledgement, thank you to my wonderful wife, Gemma. I would not be here without you, I would not be me without you, and I would not be as excited about the rest of my days if I didn't have you by my side. I love you xxx

Infinity 2012